He lives in Bloomington, Minnesota, a suburb of Minneapolis. He has lived only here, but travels everywhere. Chess, Tennis, Risk, Ping Pong, he'll take you all on. When the sun is shining and the sky is blue you'll finding him whipping around town on a bicycle. At home, though, he mimics Chloe the cat and lounges about for both believe sleep is not a waste of time. His favorite fruit is pears and he eats oatmeal like there's no tomorrow. If you want to see what he looks like check out his YouTube channel. Oh, and he has a Masters Degree from the University of St. Thomas. Anything else?

twitter: @timyearneau

www.timyearneau.com

www.facebook.com/yarndog

www.youTube.com/yarndog50

ISBN-13: 978-0-9894750-5-1
ISBN-10: 0-9894750-5-0

*Note To Self* is a work of nonfiction.
A few names have been changed for privacy reasons.


In Memory of little Chloe
R.I.P.


Cover Design by
Sorin Radulescu
upwork.com

# Note To Self

## Stream of Consciousness

Also by Tim Yearneau

# Curveballs: Sweet & Smokey Down the Barbeque Trail

# Guide to Intellectual Property

# Table of Contents

# CHAPTER 1

All I wanted to do was make my car payment. How I went so wrong I don't know. With work done for the day I hopped on my bike and spun the pedals in an easy circular motion as I began heading down the four mile stint of bike trail through breezy trees and glimmering ponds. The sunshine pouring through the blue skies filled me with all the vitamin D imaginable. Arriving at the end of the trail I strapped the bike to my car and boogied straight to a nearby coffee shop.

For me as an educator the sad fact is money is tight this time of year. It's that short, dreadful period between the last regular school year pay check and first summer school pay check. Bills pile up, but money doesn't. With the educators convention to Atlanta days away, the pressure mounted.

Acknowledging I'm to be reimbursed for my trip expense doesn't change the equation. I pay upfront and get reimbursed later. Adding to the vise, I'm leaving early before the convention starts to spend time as a tourist, meaning my own money pours from my pockets.

I calculate and re-calculate until my teeth hurt, but repeated spreadsheet calculations don't ease the stress. The next paycheck would arrive on Monday, four days away. In the meantime I'd be in Atlanta running up expenses, though having fun. The fun won't change anything either, perhaps only ratcheting up the anxieties.

Nor does rationalizing that I've taken other trips with far less coin. I once drove down to Texas with two others for a wedding. It only cost me $300 for the entire six day period, and I had the time of my life.

Considering all this I packed up my laptop, plopped in the car, and exited the parking lot heading east on 494. Exiting 10 miles later, the friendly confines of Walmart waited. I zoomed from aisle to aisle, scooping up all that would be necessary.

Somewhere during my zooms a thought coursed through my brain. *Dang it, I forgot to make my car payment.* The credit union where I make payments is near the end of the bike trail, but I forgot. And they aren't set up for online payments. Now, during rush hour, I'll have to drive all the way back, though I very much don't want to.

I pushed buttons on my cell phone, *ring, ring, ring.*

"Hello," said the voice on the other end.

"Yes, my car payment is due today. Could I pay it over the phone with my credit card?"

"We don't allow car payments with a credit card."

"Oh ... mmm, I know there is a 10 day grace period for making a payment. I'm going on a trip tomorrow morning and won't be able to get in before I leave. What's the final due date for the grace period to expire?

"June 8th."

"Oh, that's cutting it close."

Leaving the credit union and re-entering 494 east for the drive home, I encountered a murderous traffic jam. I exited onto south 169 to relieve the pressure, but the weight of tight finances still haunted me, causing my hands to clutch the steering wheel extra tight while simultaneously gritting my teeth. My forearms stiffened like wood and sweat worked its way down my brow and lip in a slow steady drip.

If my problems weren't enough, as though pouring salt on a wound, a new traffic jam took hold, far exceeding what I had left behind on 494. Cars lined up for miles. I suffocated in pity.

They say that most of life isn't fair, whoever *they* are, but I resent it being so brutal. However, my prior experience in Chicago paid dividends. I took a deep breath, giving myself permission to curse a little, while staying in the same lane. I thought about using my ingenious lane-switching algorithm, but then remembered the results achieved when I used it in St. Louis. Complete failure.

Instead I stayed calm and regained my composure, rolling the windows up, and turning on the air conditioner. I tuned in a good radio station, all the while whistling while I waited. At the precise moment I exited onto Old Shakopee Road, following the straight and narrow path to home sweet home.

\* \* \*

On other trips barbeque took a backseat to something with greater priority; The Fever in Chicago, American Idol in Los Angeles. I could use the same type of rationale here, but I won't.

I'm going to Atlanta to be a local union delegate for the National Education Association Representative Assembly convention, herein known as the NEA. This purpose alone credentials me for bailing out on barbeque with a litany of excellent excuses; *I'll be too busy, someone else is paying the freight, this is too important, there'll be conflicts with NEA events, I'll be tired.* Blah, blah, blah. All lame. I have plenty of time and I'm coming early to be Joe Tourist. As I later learned a delegate works hard, but plays hard too.

As a final excuse I wanted to be done with this book, so I rationalized that I could come back to Atlanta another time.

Besides, adding Atlanta to the Mr Y BBQ Tour would add torturous months to the editing process, sending my illusionary timeframe into oblivion.

All of this is absurd, I finally concluded. I'd be a fool if I didn't hit barbeque while in Atlanta, the heart of the Deep South, the very soul of barbeque country. I needed to take advantage of the here and now for who knows how long it might be before I would come back. Opportunity is knocking now, not tomorrow; carpe diem, dammit. I'm all in.

\* \* \*

I strolled down the concourse of the Minneapolis-St. Paul International airport at a leisurely pace. My departure gate for Atlanta graced the far end, as far as you can go, beyond the visible horizon. With not a worry in the world I glided into the concourse mini-mart and purchased some blueberry yogurt. I had left home in plenty of time, rushing out the door to avoid being a last minute casualty.

As I removed the top to the yogurt, I felt the weight of the backpack pressing down on my back. I had loaded it to the hilt, filling every spare inch. I ripped the plastic spoon from its package and dumped the mucky yogurt cover in the nearest trash bin. I took the newspaper I'd just bought, rolled it up, and tucked it under my arm. I continued to stroll down the concourse as I took sweet gulps of yogurt, all the while playing a pleasant jingle in my head. The sky looked blue and beautiful as the rays of the sun broke the clouds.

*"Passenger Tim Yearneau, this is your last boarding call for Delta Flight twelve-ninety-one. Please proceed to the gate for your last boarding call,"* a voice bellowed over the airport intercom. Son-of-a-beehive! I paused in shock.

According to the clock I witnessed a minute ago I had almost 25 minutes before boarding. Other passenger names poured out of the overhead speaker, too. I've boarded lots of airplanes before with minutes to spare and have been just fine.

Scrambling to organize I picked up the pace, taking gulps of yogurt at an ever increasing clip.

*"Passenger Tim Yearneau, this is your last boarding call for Delta Flight twelve-ninety-one. Please pro-*

ceed to the gate for your last boarding call."

Fear gripped me and I dumped the yogurt and newspaper in the trash with a one-piece motion. The potential humiliation, not to mention extra expense, motivated me as I made a quick check of the backpack for tightness of fit, bolting at full-speed like Dagwood Bumstead, sweat flying from me onto the concourse floor. Get in my way and you'll get hurt, I thought. Moving in leaps and bounds down the long and forever hallway, my bum knees didn't complain a bit.

Flying at full tilt, powered by panic, I heard it one more time, "*Passenger Tim Yearneau this is your last boarding call for Delta Flight twelve-ninety-one. Please proceed to the gate for last boarding call. This is your last call.*" I'm almost there, I thought, I'm close, don't you see me? I'm running as fast as I can. *Hang on.* Don't close that gate!

* * *

I had experienced this monstrous dilemma before. The most memorable happened a little over a dozen years ago on my way to Uzbekistan to pay a visit to Lisa Ocone. I had flown into Dulles airport in Washington, D.C., with her sister, Julie, in order to make a connecting flight to India, our first leg. We had done everything they said to do for an international flight, arriving fully 3 hours early.

As fate would have it 7 other flights arrived at the same time. Julie went ahead to the departure gate at Terminal 2, across the tarmac. Meanwhile, I zig-zagged in one of the many lines that stretched down and around the corner.

We passengers were like ants in an ant farm awaiting marching orders. Not only did I have the backpack strapped to my back, I lugged a heavy-as-a-brick suitcase earmarked for Lisa Ocone as well. Overwhelmed by the arriving flights the understaffed counter agents made heroic efforts to move passengers on to their connecting flights.

When I got to the counter I had only 20 minutes to get from there to the departure gate at Terminal 2, which I must remind you, was on the other side of the tarmac, where Julie sat waiting.

They ran my backpack through the x-ray machine and after being scanned I grabbed it for the long run to the tram. Except they made an error. I had to run it through again.

After the second scan I grabbed it again and headed off. Except I had another checkpoint to head through. From there I bolted to the tram like O.J. Simpson in a Hertz commercial.

Halfway through the slow-as-a-turtle tram ride something seemed strange. Reaching behind and tapping my back I figured it out. No backpack. All of my possessions for the entire trip lay in that backpack, which sat at the second checkpoint in the main terminal.

I could see our Boeing 747 Jumbo jetliner out the window of the tram. I fidgeted in a sweat filled panic for the tram to finish crossing the tarmac. Muttering prayers of hope didn't do a lick of good.

Arriving back at the main terminal, I sprinted like the Road Runner to the checkpoint to reclaim my backpack.

But there were more delays as I had to prove who I said I was. This subtracted precious minutes to get on that plane. When they finally let me go I grabbed my backpack with a jerk and bolted to the tram.

I stood the entire tram ride back; my anxieties having a field day. I exited in full sprint, running the corridors of Terminal 2 as fast as my legs would allow, the weight of my backpack taking its toll.

The departure gate, as fate would have it, sat on the far terminus of that long, never-ending, marathon concourse. In ok shape, but not an Olympic Athlete, I soon reached a physical limit.

Up ahead Julie urged me to the finish line, waving me on with a flurry of motion, exhorting me with all her might, "Hurry! Hurry! Run! They're closing the gate!" I walked at a brisk pace, all that I could muster and all that I had left, out of breath.

When I got to the gate, with the Boeing 747 Jumbo jetliner in full view, the agent informed me, "We've closed the gate for boarding."

"But the plane is right there!" I said.

"I'm sorry sir, we've removed the wheel blocks."

Just put the wheel blocks back, I thought. So I said, "Can't you just open the gate? The plane is right there!" My pleading was of no avail.

A group of 30 passengers on the way to their homeland in Africa were stuck like me. But they were fully paying customers while I wasn't. I held standby status due to getting my plane ticket in exchange for doing web design work for an airline employee friend of mine.

"Aren't you mad? Aren't you mad you paid full fare and they won't let you on?" I exhorted the Africans. "The plane is right there," shaking my finger at the jet that filled the window. I took note of their rising anger.

In short order they *slammed* their luggage to the ground. One of them stormed up to the ticket window and cemented his elbows on the counter demanding to know from the agent why they weren't on that flight.

I poured it on, saying to them, again, "It's right there! And they won't let you on. Aren't you mad?" I reveled inside with glee at the chaos I'd caused, all designed to convince the agents of the errors of their ways in closing that gate.

The Africans, their fury increasing to that of a raging bull, moved amongst themselves as though ready to take up arms.

*"You! Come with me!"* a voice shouted with a viciousness of volume. Not knowing where this came from I reacted by turning, only to face off with an agent shak-

ing her finger with utter violence at me, her body filled with a unique brand of rage. I knew I'd been caught, and I followed her in humility. Stopping in a bolt, and facing me square, she said, "You can't do that to us! We have enough trouble as it is! If you cause us trouble then not only will we not let you on, we'll revoke the flying privileges of the employee you got the ticket from!!!" Wow! The sheer force of her anger pounded me into submission.

My friend, the airline employee, had warned me about this very situation, and now I was seconds away from it becoming true. Full of remorse I said to the agent, in a whisper, "I'm sorry. It was a heat of the moment thing and I wanted to be on that plane and it's still right there. My friend warned me about causing trouble for him and I certainly don't want to. You have a tough situation here and I realize I'm making it worse. I'm sorry." With drooping head, I couldn't look her in the eye.

* * *

Today, in my current dilemma, sprinting down the concourse of the Minneapolis-St. Paul International Airport in order to catch Delta Flight 1291 to Atlanta, thoughts of that prior experience at Dulles Airport dominated. I continued to sprint at a desperate pace until reaching the Delta ticket counter. I couldn't help but notice the counter agent holding the mike to his face ready to declare me booted from the flight.

"I'm here! I'm here!" I yelled, nearly out of breath.

The counter agent saw me and said in a soothing calm, "You don't have to worry any more. You don't have to run. Go ahead and walk and get on the plane. There is plenty of time."

I did as he said and slowed to a walk. I said, "I heard my name and I'm like 'Oh no!' I ran full tilt and I'm out of breath. Thank you, thank you," inhaling short bursts of air. He smiled, grabbed my ticket, and scanned it. I grabbed my things, grateful as can be, and took the first steps down the runway, never looking back.

\* \* \*

I would be remiss if I didn't fill you in on the final outcome of my India flight those years ago. Julie and I did indeed miss it. They weren't about to open the doors for us. Tension and chaos continued to strafe the air. In addition to the agent's fury, Julie was none too pleased, and the Africans were still going bananas.

In the midst of this the agent started punching some buttons on her terminal. "Did you know," she said in a calm tone, "that because of the kind of ticket you have I can book you First Class on every leg of your trip, including your return flight?"

"No, I did not," I said, attempting to process this unforeseen turn of events.

"I can book you on the first flight out tomorrow."

"That would be fantastic!" I said, now beaming a broad smile, knowing that lemons had just been turned into lemonade. The Chaos Theory at work.

\* \* \*

The flight to Atlanta was uneventful, pleasant if you will. I brought a book to read, *Red Shift Blue Shift: The Pendulum of Time* by Leslie Peterson.

He is a local Minneapolis writer. It's a fun, creative sci-fi adventure story and reading it during the flight provided me great tranquility.

While sitting in my seat I couldn't help but reflect one more time about my India trip those years ago. I had pulled the thrill of victory out of the agony of defeat, and gotten more than I bargained for when the agent booked me First Class the rest of the trip. Perhaps in Atlanta, I mused, that same kind of good fortune would come tumbling down again in my search for the perfect barbeque.

Arriving in Atlanta I was struck by how big the airport is. Getting to Hertz to pick up my rental car took some navigating and a trailblazing spirit. I had to go down long corridors, up and down escalators, ride a few obscure elevators, take a train ride, and do more walking, walking and walking until I was there. Hertz has a very cheery and professional process for checking in, and in no time I exited the parking ramp in a Ford Fiesta, ready for adventure.

I had it in my mind that Hartsfield International Airport lies a dramatic distance south of downtown Atlanta. It does not. I headed north on 85, zipping by downtown in minutes, and continued on to my motel in Norcross, a northeast suburb. I exited onto a random road to ask for directions and pulled into the nearest restaurant.

I approached a waitress who, without prompting, asked me, "Where are you from?" in her beautiful Southern drawl. I love that sweet Southern accent. There's something wholesome, charming, and warm about it.

"Minneapolis. Say do you know where Indian Trail Lilburn Road is?" I couldn't help but notice her alluring attire. Knit leggings, short skirt, busty top. If I didn't know any better, I'd say I'm was in the Atlanta version of Hooters with a sprinkle of sultry.

She guided me on my way, still melting me with that sweet Southern drawl—an interesting start to an educators convention.

# CHAPTER 2

Feeling exhausted and in the throes of sinus problems, I took a nap to freshen up. Part of my fatigue came from my continued anxieties over tight finances. Repeated spreadsheet calculations came up with the same dismal numbers and it sucked the energy right out of me.

I woke up from my nap with most of the afternoon gone. I headed to the grocery store to pick up stuff for a Super Salad. I love salads and wanted to save money and eat healthy at the same time. I'd lost a bunch of weight at work during our Biggest Loser contest and I had made a commitment to a lifestyle change. It's the best I've done in terms of losing weight and keeping it off in over a dozen years.

Salads became my counterweight to eating barbeque. Let's face it: eating barbeque is a deliciously spiritual experience and good for the emotions, but it's a killer on the waistline. A little research shows that barbeque is some of the worst food on the planet for our health; high on fat, calories, cholesterol, sugar, sodium, and who knows what. In short, it's death food.

But, it came time to start the adventure with barbeque leading the charge. Research on the barbeque scene in Atlanta named popular places like Fox Bros., Fat Matt's, Heirloom, and Harold's. But I had to know where the locals went. Taking a stroll to the front desk I asked the clerk, "Hey, where's a good barbeque place around here?"

The friendly middle-aged fellow, said, "Well, I like Shane's BBQ. There's one about 6 miles from here." He pointed to the main road a short jog from the motel.

Heading back up to the room I fired up my laptop, an older MacBook Pro. I discovered Shane's is a chain of 150 restaurants, with the original one being in McDonough, Georgia, some 50 miles from Norcross. I made a blink of a decision to go there.

Franchises are great and all that, but nothing beats the original. There's always an intriguing story behind it, and the mandate that powers the Mr Y BBQ Tour is to get that story.

I plowed down 85 south for the journey to Shane's. Traffic flowed nice and smooth, except for the temporary traffic jam near downtown. Following 85 as it weaved through downtown, I caught 75 south looking for Eagles Landing Parkway exit. I found it a pounding distance south of downtown Atlanta and exited east for the drive to McDonough.

Getting there took a bit as the road alternated between urban structures, open country, more urban structures, and more open country creating a kind of disconnect for the urban traveler.

I stopped my car for the red lights that adorned the intersection where highway 155 crosses over. It's then I recognized the building sitting kitty corner from the pictures online. The road sign occupying the corner of their lot confirmed I'd arrived.

The original Shane's Ribshack is a small white country structure with a red angular roof, the kind I might find in a Norman Rockwell painting. For good measure, wooden steps lead to the front door, and a wooden walkway leads to a side door. In the truest sense, it's a hole-in-the-wall.

I entered the front door and plopped up to the red counter to place an order.

The kitchen space looked as crammed as an overstuffed closet. Architects seemingly forgot about the kitchen when they were hired to expand the premises. It's like they were under orders to keep it jammed.

At Shane's, the kitchen is hidden from view by the wall displaying the Big Red menu. The color scheme of the place is easy to describe. White with thick strokes of red. Shane's would blend in perfectly in Lincoln, Nebraska, home of the University of Nebraska Cornhuskers; Big Red territory.

At 9 pm that night, an hour before closing time, buzz and energy filled the air. From the moment I stepped in the door the constant stream of customers kept employees busy at an adrenaline-fueled clip. I scoured their menu and went for the traditional half-slab ribs, corn on the cob, French fries, baked beans, and Brunswick stew. The last item raised the bar on my curiosity.

I hounded the clerk, a short, blond, college-aged woman, wearing a Shane's t-shirt and baseball hat, "Are you camera shy? I'm from out of town. I love barbeque ribs and whenever I go on trips I hit rib places and interview people and post little YouTube videos. I'm writing a travelogue book on all of it too. Are you open to being on-camera?"

She said, "No I'm not camera shy, but the owner's daughter is in the back."

My eyes shot big, "Oh, that would be great!"

"She's busy now, but I'll talk to her and let her know you're here."

"Fantastic." Game on. I headed out to the screened porch area and immediately recruited a family eating there to film me as I made a glorious Mr Y BBQ Tour introduction.

In a flash a server arrived with my order. It came t*hat* fast.

I grew anxious on the inside, ready to bug the server about the owner's daughter, but held back reasoning she'd fill me in when she had good news about my request. A short while later my server stopped by again to check on things.

My impatience proved too much, "Did you talk to the

daughter?"

"She's still busy." My nervousness increased as the clock on the wall now read 9:30 pm. Please, I thought, please let this interview happen.

Hungry, I dug in. The atmosphere out there had the feel of a cabin in the woods, and it sang with the bouncy jibe of the honky tonk Cajun music playing overhead.

I started with the sides and worked my way up to the ribs. Being honest I rate the French fries as average. The baked beans were respectable and held their own. The corn-on-the-cob good, as corn-on-the-cob by its very nature is good. The Brunswick stew would have to wait.

During Cow Week at my student's culinary course at Hennepin Technical College in Eden Prairie, Minnesota, I learned there are multiple ways to make barbeque ribs. They can be boiled, baked or smoked.

The ribs I ate at Shane's were either baked or boiled, I couldn't tell which. All I know is that the light-brown muddy colored meat fell off the bone *sooooo* easy and the texture *sooooo* tender. Dang it was good. Part of the fun is trying the sauces and they didn't disappoint: Original, Spicy, Mustard, and Hot.

In mathematical terms the sauces had a narrow standard deviation from the mean. In more verbose terms, on the high end of the spectrum, Hot brought the heat, but it wouldn't power a furnace and knock me on my pants. It'd be a climb to the mountain top for the novice, but a walk in the park to the hardcore. I'm a brave soul and willing to be daring, but I don't want to have to call the fire department.

Spicy wasn't hot. No siree Bob.

But it did have a twangy kick that lingered, which separated it from the crowd. The word Spicy inherently implies a bite that grips, but doesn't hurt. It makes a statement, but doesn't light a match.

The Mustard sauce is really Mustard lite. It was flavorful enough to be noticed, but not enough to cause me a tortured face.

Original could very easily be named Neutral. A slight bend towards sweet, putting an overt emphasis on slight. To borrow a term from the Intelligence community, it is the Safe House of their sauces.

For those who come to Shane's expecting their sauces to follow a scorched earth policy, they'll be disappointed. For those who are looking for their sweet tooth to go bananas, forget it. No trip to the dentist will be necessary.

Non-extremists like me find Shane's to be the perfect place. Their sauces fit a narrow range, befitting a narrow standard deviation from the mean. I want to have my cake and eat it too.

To summarize, the Hot on one end gave me a chance to be daring without the worry of it ending badly. Original on the other end satisfied my sweet tooth, but avoided being over the top. The bottom line was that wimps like me walked away happy.

The waitress never did come back and give me an update on the daughter, so I took matters into my own hands. I walked into the main entry area, the crossroads of the structure if you will, and waited. Patience is a virtue and I had a lot of it. Customers kept coming, one after another, in onesies and twosies, and in groups, but always a line. I intended for the line to come down, and then pounce.

A taller 6'3" middle-aged white gentleman paced back and forth, looking out the windows with a nervous tick, checking the clock as though in a hurry.

Dressed in a dark blue polo shirt and tan pants, he checked the doors, and at one point stopped his pacing long enough to flick off the OPEN sign.

Sitting one chair over from me was Shawn, an African-American man with a heavier than average build, wearing a blue mechanics shirt. He had moved to Atlanta from Chicago a number of years ago. I made easy conversation with him which soon turned towards his newest passion, barbeque. He dreamed of opening his own barbeque place someday.

"Did you know Shane's offers franchises? Look, it says so right on the cup," I told him matter-of-factly.

Shawn looked at the cup in his hand and raised his eyebrows. The Truth stared him in the face, "No, I didn't."

"Barbeque is competitive." I said. "Everyone's got an ego, but it's a fun ego. No one is out to harm anyone else."

"Yeah, I know," he said. "Me and my brother compete with each other all the time over whose barbeque is better."

"Hey, are you camera shy? Could I interview you for my camera? I like to make little YouTube videos and post them."

Shawn said, "I'm still working on my barbeque skills. Besides I'm shy. I have to work on my skills and build my confidence." I sensed that a lack of confidence in his barbeque skills presented a hefty roadblock to opening his own place.

"You know it's funny," I said "I love to eat barbeque, but I'm just a consumer. I don't actually make it. I should try and make some ribs sometime, and come up with my own secret sauce like everybody else. That would be half the fun."

"You should, it would be fun," Shawn said. He grabbed his order, said his goodbyes and headed out the door.

My conversation with him lasted but a fleeting moment, but I had met another kindred spirit, another member of the fraternity, and that's all that mattered.

Still waiting for the line to die down and for the daughter to show herself, I schmoozed with the tall gentleman still pacing to and fro like an expectant father. Curiosity popped as to why he flipped the switch on the

OPEN sign. Most customers wouldn't take it upon themselves to do such a thing, but he didn't look like an employee either.

"The line never slows down does it?" I asked him.

"No, it never does. That's why I had to turn off the sign and lock the doors. If I don't, the customers keep coming. The workers want to go home too," he said, with a friendly smile. I still puzzled for an explanation as to who this man was. Soon it became apparent from the shiny badge on his shirt.

"I'm from out of town and love barbeque. I bring my camera everywhere I go and do interviews and make little YouTube videos. I'm writing a book too. My waitress explained the owner's daughter is here tonight and I'm waiting to talk to her when it's not so busy."

"Oh, that's great. Where are you from?"

"I'm from Minneapolis." I started in, "The last time I was in Atlanta was in 1996 when I came for the Olympics. Everyone is so hospitable here. That's one of the biggest things I remember about Atlanta. Everyone rolled out the red carpet and laid on the Southern hospitality. It was wonderful. I came with my brother and his kid and we camped way up in Dahlonega. I just remember the Southern hospitality." I butchered my pronunciation of Dahlonega, pronouncing it *Duh-LA-ga-na*.

"Oh sure, Dahlonega," he said, pronouncing it the right way, *Da-len-ega*. "Well, you came to the right place. It's like that here. Everyone in these parts are so friendly and will roll out the red carpet for you."

"Are you camera shy?"

"No, no, no, I don't want to be on camera. I'm not dressed for it and I don't like to be on camera, especially since I'm working. Here let me give you a tour." By now I had figured it out. He worked as a local officer-of-the-law, on duty at Shane's.

Why do they need a Police Officer at Shane's, I wondered. Is it dangerous? Am I in a bad area? Those thoughts faded quickly, as I recognized Shane's had a boatload of cash on-hand after a busy non-stop day of business. It made sense.

If he didn't have that badge on his shirt identifying him as an officer-of-the-law, I would think he was a personal concierge hired by Shane's. I got a wonderful earful on the short history of Shane's, which I soaked up with the curiosity of a first-grader learning the alphabet for the first time.

Next, he walked outside and gave me a rundown on three different outdoor seating options. The first, a screened porch, "is covered with windows in the winter." The second, a permanently enclosed area, " is air-conditioned for summertime comfort." The third, an open air deck, "didn't used to be this big. A year earlier a car careened off Highway 155 and destroyed it. Shane's took this as an opportunity to expand it." They did a good job.

Walking down the steps to the playground, the officer-of-the-law gloated, "Most places don't even have a playground, much less a big beautiful one like this. This is what separates Shane's from everyone else. They do everything first class. They are great people, that family."

Back in the crossroads area he pointed to a frame on the wall holding a photograph of a love letter Shane's wife wrote to Shane.

The officer-of-the-law explained, "They love each other so much, and it shows in how this place is run and how they treat their employees and their customers.

They give back to the community with all their heart and they are just wonderful to have here. You'll never meet a better family. We're lucky to have them in our community."

Next, he gave me a mini-tour of the ordering area and filled me in on more Shane's history. I knew, listening to him, I'd scored gold. I never thought those warm fuzzy feelings from 1996 could ever be replicated. I was wrong.

chapter 2

Southern hospitality isn't a fad that withers with time. It strengthens like a hurricane as time marches forward. It creates happiness and warm feelings, and reconnects us to a better way, leaving the recipient full of gratitude to have experienced it, and questioning why there are divides in this world. If life has got you down make it easy on yourself. Come to the South, rejuvenate your soul, and let your faith be restored in your fellow man.

"Shane's is first class in everything, even their outhouse is air conditioned," the officer-of-the-law said with oozing pride.

A tiny white structure with the word OUTHOUSE plastered across the top was unavoidable as one walked up the wooden walkway to the side entrance of Shane's. It's black angled roof mimicked the angular shape of the main building.

"Come with me, I'll show you," he said. He opened the door to the outhouse and I took a single step in.

The tiny structure approximated the size of a walk-in closet, enough room for a sink and a toilet. Turning my head slightly to the left I observed the air conditioning unit doing what it was designed to do.

"See, only at Shane's. They do everything first class," he said, with a smile working overtime. Amazed and speechless, I couldn't disagree.

Heading back in to the main building, I asked, "Are you from around here?"

Standing like two friends having a chat, he said, "No. I'm originally from New Jersey."

"Do you go back to visit very often?"

"Not real often, every once in a while."

"I heard you mention something about vacation and fishing."

"I'm going on vacation to Sea Island next week off the coast of Georgia for a little fishing. I love to fish. I made a deal with another officer that if I work his shift this week he'll cover me next week. I can't wait."

"Sounds fun. I'm not a big fishing kind of guy, but just getting out there away from the rat race is fun all by itself. Just the act of casting the line is relaxing."

"Oh yeah! It'll be fun to get away. I know what you mean."

With the doors locked and no more customers streaming in, the daughter finally appeared at the counter. Two daughters actually—Shaina and Summer. Both white Caucasian and college-aged, but with divergent paths. One wore a baseball hat. The other, a head band. Despite their differences, it was easy to tell they were sisters.

They were willing participants in my scheme, answering my swarm of questions with precision. Shaina was the more outgoing of the two and did most of the talking. I scored the scoop on Shane's I'd dreamed about, my mandate satisfied.

"Do you like sweet tea, would you like some?" Summer offered with a cheery smile at the end of the night.

"Yes, I love tea."

"Great, here you go." She handed me a one-gallon jug. I had expected a glass, but this is the South.

"Did you try our peach cobbler? It's one of our specialties," Shaina insisted.

"No, I didn't. That's one thing I didn't get. I'm too full. But what the heck, who can say no?"

She reappeared moments later with a large styrofoam container packed tight with peach cobbler. I made a deal with myself to save it and try it back at the motel. Portion control. I left Shane's with an overbearing feeling of warmth; Southern hospitality was alive and kicking. It's the gift that keeps on giving.

When I pulled into the parking lot of my motel in Norcross at 11:45 pm, I knew I'd be so pumped with adrenaline I wouldn't be able to sleep right away. I rushed up to the room, unpacked the laptop, hooked up the camera, fired up iMovie and went to work. After loading the footage I pushed the spacebar to start playing the clip, waiting in silent anticipation.

"*NOOOOOO!*" I screamed, stopping the clip. I checked my connections, and pushed the spacebar again. "*NOOOOOO!*" The adrenaline thing started to wear off. I sat and stared at the screen, running through the possibilities.

After some mental calisthenics I determined it had to be the settings on the camera. I spent the next hour checking every possible setting on both the camera and laptop. I even pulled the batteries out and theorized about them. Nothing I did changed the outcome. I came to the awful conclusion *I'm screwed*. I had great video, but no sound. My Interview of the Century was now a silent movie.

I toyed with the idea of leaving it that way. I could add subtitles and pattern it after the silent movies of the Roaring 20s. I even pulled up some on YouTube and examined them. No, I concluded, after much consideration, I'm not going to do it. The flavor of my interview would be lost. It would take a lot of work for it to make sense, and my small time audience deserves better. I had paid an unfair price for my bad habit of leaving the camera in the car. The humid, scorching hot Minnesota summers torched it. The brutal winters froze the bytes out of it.

I needed a working camera for the rest of my trip. Like Albert Einstein, I used thought experiments to find a solution. I liked the Kodak Playsport, but money was tight and I hadn't worked unplanned expenses into my budget.

There are limits. My finances needed to be a zero sum game. The extra expense for a new camera over here had to come out of a bucket over there.

Salads. I would munch on extra salads and eat out less. That's how I kept my trip under $300 those years ago, buying more from the grocery store and eating less at fast-food places and fancy restaurants.

I searched online for Best Buy stores in the greater Atlanta area. I searched their website and determined a brand new Kodak Playsport camera would run me $145. I racked my brain. *Aha!* Craigslist. I searched the listings for used Kodak Playsport cameras and found two for sale, one listed in Alpharetta and the other in Macon. Time for bed.

# CHAPTER 3

I awoke at 10 am. My grocery store purchases paid dividends. Bowl, check. Plastic spoon, check. Salad, check. Cereal, check. Fruit, check. Yogurt, check. I ate like a king. In between bites I placed impatient phone calls to Alpharetta and Macon.

I left and headed to Planet Fitness. Working out builds my ego. When I tell someone "I worked out," I'm bragging. I pretend I'm not, but I am. I'm a competitor and I'm always searching for an edge. This is one way I do it.

"Do you know where the nearest Best Buy is around here? I know there's one around somewhere," I asked the front desk clerk.

"You want to know where the nearest Best Buy is?" she asked.

"Yes."

"Give me one second, I'll print you out a map." Now wait a minute ... I didn't expect this. In Minnesota they would tell me the address and directions verbally. But I'm in the South! She came back and handed me a nice Google map, clear as a clean window. I left to do my workout.

In the middle of my workout I heard the faint *ring, ring, ring* of my phone. Scrambling, I pulled it out and pushed the green answer button, whipping it to my ear.

"Hello."

"Yes, you called about the Playsport I had for sale on Craigslist?"

"Yes I did. You wanted $60 for it?" I readied myself to enter intense negotiations to get the price down. I had turned cheap, a byproduct of tight finances. Every mention of the almighty dollar became an exercise in stress and worry. It's also in my DNA. If I can get the sucker down a buck, I win.

"Yes $60," Brian said.

"I'll take it. What's your address?"

I finished my workout, showered up, and approached the front desk. "How do I get to Alpharetta?"

"Do you have an address? I'll print you up a map."

"Yes."

She came back with another beautiful Google map and informed me Alpharetta was a 30 mile drive, at least. She wasn't kidding. I drove and drove. I passed the time reminiscing about 1996 again.

Pete, his son Chris, and I drove 26 hours straight from Minneapolis to Atlanta in my old beater tan Ford Econoline van. It was a stick shift with two gas tanks. I drove the first leg and woke them hours later at the Indy 500 racetrack in Indianapolis, Indiana, the first time they'd ever been there.

We camped at Amicalola Falls State Park near Dahlonega, 75 miles northeast of Atlanta. Dahlonega is the site of the first gold rush in the United States. It happened a long time ago, in 1828, to be exact. For history buffs like me the Dahlonega Gold Museum Historic site still graces the center of town square.

By the grace of God's beauty Amicalola Falls State Park was and is one of the most gorgeous places on earth. To register for our campground we had to drive up a steep one mile drive to the main lodge. Road signs warned us of the steep ascent we were about to embark on. Make sure your brakes are good, the sign warned. If the brakes are bad, good luck, fella.

I put that old Hog in first gear and stomped on the accelerator, feeling the *whhrrrrr* and grind of the engine as it used all it's might to take us to the top.

All three of us watched the heat gauge in a nail biter.

We couldn't afford to blow a gasket or shoot a rod.

We frequented a particular restaurant close to Dahlonega, near the small town of Dawsonville. It's the red carpet treatment by the owner of that restaurant that got burned into my brain all these years. It's his treatment of us I remember when I tell those who'll listen to me about the Southern hospitality I experienced back then. I can still visualize our conversations with him. He always had a pot of coffee in his hand. And each and every time he laid the hospitality on thick. I don't remember the name of that restaurant, for back in 1996 I was just going to the Olympics, not writing a book!

A redeeming feature of those Olympics was the army of vendors occupying downtown Atlanta, hawking everything in sight. The world's newspapers were critical, saying that Atlanta was too capitalistic and not enough Olympic spirit. Americans only cared about making a buck, they said. Well, we *are* capitalists. We hawk. We sell. We hustle. We want that buck. That's *who* we are. When in Rome do as the Romans!

Even way back in 1996 The Fever found his way into my Olympic moment. I worked a bunch of odd jobs for extra money, including working with him cleaning a health club one night a week during the graveyard shift. Yes, The Fever was my boss. To say he was a slave driver wouldn't do it justice.

Pete called on that Friday. "I got tickets to the Olympics. It starts Monday. Do you want to go?"

"Yes."

But a problem persisted. I tried to contact the head health club boss for permission to miss work, but got his voice mail and left a message. I heard back from him on that Monday while in Atlanta. He said he understood, not a problem. When I got back from the Olympics I showed up for my shift at the health club.

The Fever shuffled back and forth mumbling, but I couldn't understand a word he said. I told him, "Fever, speak up, I can't understand a word you're saying."

"You didn't have to come in tonight," he mumbled.

"What? What do you mean I don't have to come in tonight? I'm scheduled."

The Fever drooped his head and shuffled back and forth, like he did in Chicago, except without the stomp or brood, "Not any more. The boss was unhappy about this Olympic thing. You don't have to come anymore," barely saying it in a whisper.

"What? I'm fired? You're firing me?"

The Fever continued to shuffle back and forth, head drooping, and pushing his broom. "Yes," he whispered.

"Are you kidding me? He said it was okay over the phone and now he says it isn't? Forget it. I'm not making much anyways. I get paid dog wages and I only work a couple of hours a week. Ha ha ha ha. He's making you do the dirty work. You're firing me! Ha ha ha ha!"

"Ha ha ha ha," The Fever bellowed, pouring it on, "I'm firing you. Ha ha ha ha. You're fired!!"

"Screw it. Start up the whirlpool Fever. I need to re-lax." And The Fever did.

* * *

Here and now, I exited the main freeway onto curvy, windy, skinny, hallow country roads. I overshot turns, overran intersections, and doubted myself. I wondered if Google Maps sometimes got it wrong. But I lucked out. I found the neighborhood I was looking for. Homes for sale in that area were in the $300-$400k range. In Minneapolis they'd be $600-$900k easy. The street leading to where Brian lived looked similar to the country roads that got me there; curvy, windy, skinny, and hallow.

The homes in his cul-de-sac were all custom built. Each had lush green lawns, outlined in trimmed hedges with colorful flowers and plush gardens to boot. Some were colonial brick, my favorite, where others had custom wood siding. Beamers and Mercedes jammed the driveways.

The sun shone extra bright. My self-esteem took a boost for the better, my energy level rose, and I got a bit giddy on the bright side. In this neighborhood the sky is bluer, the lawns are greener, the driveways blacker, the brick browner, the siding more exotic, and the glare of the cars more distinguished. It's like the gods bought an extra special flashlight from Home Depot and illuminated the neighborhood with it.

A large semi tractor-trailer crowded Brian's driveway. Weather-beaten immigrants hauled furniture down the steel ramp up to the front door. They spoke in rapid-fire Spanish, and had all the appearances of illegal immigrants who had just crossed the border; cheap labor. Spotting Brian was easy. He stood out like a sore thumb: white, male, squeaky clean, corporate executive type.

I followed him up to his house. He spoke to the workers in his version of Spanglish. He made gallant attempts to get them to understand that he didn't want the dresser hauled into the house. When that didn't work, he tried hand motions and simple English words. "Stop. No. Stop. Put it down. Here. Put down. Here. Down, "pointing towards the ground.

I followed him inside to his office. I drooled every step of the way. Those custom white tan walls, floors made of rich dark hardwood, large see-through windows, custom trim everywhere. I knew better, but I did it anyways. I compared myself to him, which is never a good idea.

Soon, I launched an attack on the moral high ground I attempted to occupy. I concluded that this attitude of the less I have the more saintly I am is highly overrated. Brian seemed to debunk the notion that in order to be happy I have to be poor. Nothing I saw there convinced me otherwise. He didn't seem evil because he had money. In fact, he seemed like a nice cordial fellow.

Feeling the need to impress him, as I knew my 2008

Ford Focus wouldn't, I regaled him with my stories of the Mr Y BBQ Tour, filling him with details of my stop in St. Louis, the city he had moved from. This did not appear to impress him. Perhaps when the movie comes out.

Sitting in my car after paying him, the conspirator in me had doubts my original camera was actually broken. Surely it was a fluke of nature that it didn't work. I fussed and fiddled with it again. Nope, I was wrong. Buying from Brian was a smart move.

I took an alternate route back to Norcross. Back at the motel, tired, I took a nap and awoke at 4:30 pm, most of the day blown. I headed south on 85 with a game plan in mind. I'd head downtown to do tourist things and if I had time I'd head out to McDonough again for a second interview at Shane's. I had studied the maps before leaving and planned to take a shortcut via I-675.

Not too far down 85, I came upon the exit sign for I-675, situated above the far left lane, with a pointing arrow. I hauled donkey stool over there preparing to exit, but the exit never came.

In Atlanta, just because the exit sign is above the far left lane doesn't mean a thing. I still exit from the far right lane. Intellectually I came to understand this, but couldn't overcome my Minneapolis habits.

I continued to rumble south on 85. Soon orange signs warned of upcoming road work, encouraging us to take alternate routes. *Bah.* It was a Saturday afternoon, a non-work day. How bad could it be, I thought.

I choked on my vomit when I saw how long the jam up would actually be. *Feces!*

I invoked emergency measures learned from my experience in Chicago; stay in my lane, windows up, air conditioning on, tune in a good radio station and repeat to myself, "It is what it is."

Other motorists clutched their steering wheels like bandits after a bank heist. They whipped their heads in every direction, looking for a sliver of opportunity to switch lanes and get ahead. Except it didn't work. Switching lanes became their curse, leading me to think with glee, "You Fools!"

Traffic jams offer a sub-culture of the human condition. It doesn't matter if I'm rich or poor or whether I'm driving a Beamer or a Buick, I'm not moving any faster. Everyone has their own conspiracy theory on getting ahead in a traffic jam. It's like we're in a contest, and whoever can move a few inches faster gets the imaginary prize.

What will we do with the time saved? I observed Moms making vain attempts to find an open space, hoping it would make a difference to their screaming child on the way to the babysitter. It didn't. Couples fretted. Workers changed gears and accelerated, desperate to get to work on time. None of this mattered.

Dad took the worst beating as the wife was pissed and the kids frolicked in the back seat. Beads of sweat roamed his cheeks as he searched for an opening. He dropped his head and turned it away a little, like a boxer avoiding a blow, as he tried to hold off the verbal onslaught. When he made his move he hoped it would save him. But it didn't. He went down in flames anyway.

Everyone talked and texted in flurries, as though it mattered. Technology did not save them. They all chomped on the leftovers in their McDonald's bag and threw the refuge out the window at random intervals. None of this changed their status. They were stuck. It's that simple.

No matter what we think, plan or do, we're not going to move any faster. We act clever, develop anxieties, exhibit road rage; it makes no difference. We pray, plead, and curse; it makes no difference.

Solid tension hung in the air. A person of opportunity, an entrepreneur, could have made a small fortune selling high blood pressure pills. Out in the sub-culture of the jammed up freeway we need them.

One enterprising soul had the right idea. Lying in the passenger seat of a Ford Mustang he stuck his feet out the window in the manner of a leisurely Saturday afternoon stroll. What a smart man.

After an hour of being stuck in the sub-culture of nothingness I had doubts. I hemmed and hawed about going to Shane's, my resolve weakening. I had much to do; see the Martin Luther King National Historic Site, visit the Carter Center, go to the Atlanta Cyclorama Civil War museum.

I don't like to make calls on my cell phone when driving; it's too dangerous. There are more accidents from motorists on their cell phone than from drunk driving. But being stuck in that traffic jam didn't qualify as driving. I pulled out my cell phone and made the call to Shane's.

I talked to Shaina and explained my dilemma. She was working today, but not Sunday or Monday. I couldn't chance it. The NEA convention started on Monday and I lost my rental car then too. After saying our goodbyes traffic picked up a notch. I noticed a movie theater on the frontage road and made a mental note to go see *White House Down*.

Traffic returned to normal after an hour-and-a-half. The cause of the jam up was that they were building an overpass, and a big crane or machine or whatever was on the shoulder. That's it, that's what caused all the mess. Stupid, I thought.

I followed the S-curve 85 makes through downtown and passed the exit for the Georgia World Congress Center, where the NEA is held. Soon, I passed Turner Field to my left and Underground Atlanta to my right, releasing more warm fuzzy thoughts of 1996.

I connected to I-75 and made it 10 more miles before being forced to stop on a dime, stuck again right in the middle of the freeway; another full-fledged traffic jam. *Please, dear God, help me.*

Traffic jams in Atlanta, I learned, are never small affairs. They all appear to be the same size and length. Long, drawn out, and miserable. In this traffic jam, a mystery appeared. Two cars stopped solid in the middle of the freeway, one red, the other blue. Two ladies stood on the freeway amidst the stoppage. One white. One black. One spoke on her cell phone while the other held a blue gas can.

Now for the mystery. They weren't the actual traffic jam, only a sideshow. Cars crawled around them like water diverts around a stone in the middle of the river. It made sense to me that someone (*not me*) should push them to the side of the road. I crawled past them and looked in the rear view mirror. The one kept yakking on her cell phone while the other continued to stand motionless with the blue gas can in her hand.

I didn't have any idea what really caused the traffic jam. I couldn't see that far ahead. Nobody could. Doubts surfaced about my ability to get to Shane's before closing time, and exhaustion soon took hold.

I escaped along the curvy exit like a good soldier, creeping behind the motorists in front of me up onto the bridge crossing over the freeway. When I reached the other side I pulled into a taco place attached to a gas station.

"Do you know how to get to highway 155?" I asked the clerk at the counter.

"I'm sorry, I don't," he said, "let me ask somebody else," taking my order for a taco and stepping away. I hounded another employee, but he didn't know either.

Another customer entered, representing my last ray of hope. The truth is I didn't know if he was a he or a she; older, wire rimmed glasses, hair protruding from a fisherman's hat, and possessing a skinny rail of a frame.

"Excuse me, do you know how to get to highway 155 from here?" I asked, still pondering the gender of this person. "I'm trying to avoid the traffic jam on the freeway and I'm looking for an alternate route." My struggle to know the gender brought a small measure of embarrassment. It's like when someone comes up to me and talks to me like they know me, but I don't have a clue as to who they are, and I attempt to identify who they are without giving away the fact I don't know.

"I'm just passing through on my way to Kentucky," the person answered, "I don't know. I got a radiator shoot'n steam. Sorry I can't help you." Putting all the clues together, I think I figured out the gender.

I didn't get any farther next door. I asked the attendant and younger black customer for directions. The customer theorized I could take the frontage road and avoid traffic. His acquaintance, an older gentleman, took charge with more authority, "Take this frontage road," pointing to the road by the stoplight, "all the way up to Old Dixie and you'll be able to get back on 75 and avoid the traffic."

"Suckers!" I yelled out my window at the poor slobs stuck in the traffic jam. I knew they couldn't hear me, but so what. I not only won the battle, I won the war, too. I was moving and they weren't. I got to unlock my inner self and release the freedom. They were stuck. "Suckers!" I yelled one more time, pushing the button on the car door and raising the window.

I got back on 75, exited at Eagles Parkway Landing, and retraced familiar territory.

I exploded in relief when I finally entered Shane's small parking lot. I felt like I had just made a fourth quarter comeback with under two minutes to go.

Shaina and Summer saved the day with their cheery dispositions. Sherman may have made his famous March to the Sea, breaking the will of the people as he brought down carnage, but he didn't make a dent in Southern hospitality. Nope, General Sherman, you didn't make a dent.

Energized, I got right to work. "Hi from the Mr Y

BBQ Tour ... you're Shaina and you're Summer," I pointed to each them for the benefit of my small viewing audience. As before they shared equally in the smiles, but Shaina did the talking:

Mr Y: What's the Shane's story?

Shaina: Dad worked at a hospital as a nurse. Mom worked there too as an x-ray Technician. That's how they met. Dad went on to work at a heart monitor company. He got sick and tired of the corporate life and decided to make a break for it.

He up and quit and opened up this barbeque place in 2002. He had no business experience whatsoever. None. He found this place, where we are standing now, and leased it out.

It was an old little run down place, white with red roof. Over time we bought it. What we are standing in was added to over time; the porch, the outdoor deck, and the enclosed area. That's part of the charm of this place, it's the original. It's still has all the character. The first day we opened for business there was a line out the door, and we sold out.

Mr Y: I'm jealous! Who did what in the beginning?

Shaina: My mom handled all the customer service and took orders while dad worked in back making ribs.

Mr Y: Looking down the road will you both work in the family business?

Shaina: Summer works here in the summer, but that's it. She is going to school for neonatal nursing. I want to stay with the family business. I'm the manager of this store and I plan on being here a long time.

Mr Y: Has Shane's always been a franchise business and how did that get started?

Shaina: No. After about 4 years customers kept approaching us about franchise opportunities, so we decided to go for it. Right now there are about 100 Shane's BBQ Ribshack stores that stretch from the east coast all the way to Arizona. All of them are franchises except for the 4 family-owned restaurants. They aren't part of the corporation, they're family owned. All in Henrietta County. We are expanding, too.

Mr Y: How do you find franchisees? What kind of marketing do you do?

Shaina: We take out advertisements in the newspaper and book TV ads. We also have an ad on each of our cups, advertising franchising opportunities. We get a lot of our franchisees just from this. Not anyone can own a franchise. They have to go through an application process and qualify. If they do qualify they have to go through training right here in this store.

Mr Y: I noticed the other day my order came super quick. I had barely ordered and *wham*, it was there. Everyone here is so friendly and has that Southern hospitality, and lays out the red carpet. I had last been to Atlanta in 1996 and that is the one thing I distinctly remember, the Southern hospitality. Do orders always come this quick?

Shaina: That's something we pride ourselves on and we really focus on customer service. We hire people with friendly personalities who will maintain their friendliness to customers even if they are having a bad day.

Mr Y: What's your best seller? What do people go for?

Shaina: We sell a lot of chicken tenders, believe it or not. We sell lots of other stuff, too, but we sell a lot of tenders. We have a lot of schools near here. There are 4 elementary schools alone near here. People don't always want to spend a lot of money, and ribs cost a lot more, so they get the tenders. A lot of young people come through here.

Mr Y: I asked you before what your favorite food item is on the menu, and you told me the Loaded Potato. What is a Loaded Potato?

Shaina: It's new. We sell a lot of them. It's like this big (she held her hands far apart). It's got butter, nacho cheese, barbeque pork or chicken, jalapeños, sour cream, and barbeque sauce.

Mr Y: What exactly is Brunswick stew? Is it a Southern thing? I've never seen it before, but I've seen it all over down here.

Shaina: It is a Southern thing. It has a tomato base, barbeque sauce, barbeque pork, corn, black pepper—I always have to think about it—but that's about it.

With that fine piece of information I wrapped up my interview, satisfied I got it right this time. The technology worked and I got great answers to my timeless questions.

# CHAPTER 4

I pulled onto highway 155 north and accelerated. I couldn't resist the urge to experience the pure beauty of long soulful Georgia country roads. A few miles further I spotted it, a big white tent, set up in the parking lot of a gas station. Barbeque. I pulled in full of hope, but they were closed (note to self ... *Thelma's Kitchen*).

A few more miles down the road I spotted another barbeque place. This time it was a stand-alone restaurant. I pulled in there full of hope, too. But I was already full (note to self...*Pit Boss BBQ*).

I found serenity among the green forested trees, the scent of the open country, and the pace of life slowing to a manageable pause. A degree of exhaustion became a concern, the result of fending off two traffic jams. I grew in desire to see *White House Down* at that movie theater right off of 85, near Norcross. In tired times I head to the movies to unwind.

I arrived at a juncture in the road and made a blink-of-an-eye decision, heading on 275 east rather than 275 west. After I drove for a long time I began to notice the sun setting on the horizon. This went counterintuitive to my expectations. I passed a road sign which confirmed my intuition. It said: HARTSFIELD INTERNATIONAL AIRPORT—a clue to something gone awry.

Soon, the blissful peace I had enjoyed disappeared in a sea of anxieties. I had to come to grips with reality. I was headed in the wrong direction, away from Norcross rather than towards it, a simple mistake with exhausting consequences. Accepting my situation, I grew in determination to see *White House Down*.

I'd just grin and bear it and be there in time. I really had accomplished nothing on my agenda for the day. Heading to McDonough sure chewed up time. My modus operandi is to live in a state of constant *rush, rush, rush,* always regulated by an agenda. I entered 85 north, stepped on the gas, and cruised to downtown.

Coming off the final curve through downtown my fingers dug into the steering wheel. I clenched my jaw and stomped on the brakes. My Ford Fiesta jerked as it came to a sudden stop. For the third and perhaps most excruciating time that day I found myself on the rear end of a life-sucking traffic jam.

A large movie theater complex loomed across the freeway, on the edge of downtown. Not the one I was looking for, but it would do. But I saw no obvious way to get there. Going in and out of consciousness, my Chicago experience couldn't save me. I lost the patience to consider it.

Up ahead the freeway split in two, and the traffic after the right split soared along another freeway like a dream. Except I remained at the far left, with an army of steel and rubber blocking my way. My split-second decision making, my blink, failed me.

And then I saw him, a black SUV in the same predicament, make his move. Cutting his way at a right angle across lanes of traffic he honked and waved and smiled in sincere appreciation as we all let him go by.

He entered the free flow of the far right split and soared into the nighttime, skirting the agony the rest of us endured. I admired his courage and risk-taking. He was free as a bird and I was trapped in hell.

And then it happened again. A stalled car in the middle of the freeway with traffic diverting around it on both sides like water around a stone in the middle of a river. By now perhaps an Atlanta tradition.

And it wasn't the cause of the traffic jam either, only an inconvenience. Somebody (*not me*) should push that guy off to the side of the road, I thought.

It's then I saw the flashing lights of the Georgia Highway Patrol scoot up the shoulders on their way to the accident site. I stayed in my lane, crawling along. Eventually I made it to the scene.

The flashing lights of the patrol cars marked the sight like a beacon in the night. I observed a couple of destroyed cars pushed to the shoulder. Somebody heard my wails. Tow trucks readied themselves to haul away the wreckage. I had an ounce of gratitude, but only an ounce, glad I wasn't in that mess. It wasn't a pretty sight as both cars were crunched to the max.

I had spent more time in traffic jams, three to be exact, than anything else. The only thing that I'd accomplished today had been a second interview with the daughters at Shane's, and that wasn't even on my agenda. My day had been reduced to measuring the paint lines on the freeway and calculating the distance between them.

I decided to cheer up. Time for the movie! I knew the theater was off the frontage road, sandwiched between the Shallowford and Doriaville exits. I came to the first of those exits and headed down the frontage road. I'm good at persuasion and I used those skills to convince myself I was heading down the wrong track. So I reversed course and re-entered the freeway, exiting at the second of those two exits, where a colorful Caribbean bar and restaurant greeted me.

I made a right off the exit and took a right at the very next stoplight, convinced this had to be the frontage road leading to the theater. I've got the directional instincts of a bat, blessed with a radar that allows me to find what other men cannot.

I found myself in a tangled web of roads that circled, surrounded, and circumvented Mercer University. Every road had a name related to the University. I arrived at a T in the road with a decision to make, left or right? I made a decision and it was wrong. I reversed back to the T and got back on the original road. I had planned to continue past the stoplight where I made my original turn. Success is all about reversing course I reasoned. If one way doesn't work, the other will.

I zipped through the intersection, past that stoplight, confident I had corrected course. I drove along more curvy roads with names also connecting them to the university, slipping one way, then veering another, sometimes crossing over the white dashed lines that separated the lanes.

Somewhere in there another T in the road presented itself. I made another split-second decision and just *knew* glory lay around the corner. I found glory all right. All I had done was made one gigantic loop all the way back to where I had exited the freeway, where the colorful Caribbean bar and restaurant still greeted me.

I *must* try again, I thought. This string of bad luck can't stop me. I'm nothing if not persistent. I drove across the bridge to the frontage road on the other side, hung a left, and continued down to the first freeway exit. I waited patiently for the stoplight to turn green.

How come those other cars don't have to wait like I do, I thought. Unfair. Why do they get to swing right around onto the frontage road? My Fiesta made a quick jerk as I cut into their lane and followed the car in front. I cranked on the steering wheel while my tires squealed as they grabbed at the cement.

With the U-turn in the rearview mirror I stomped on the gas, nervous the movie have already started. In another blink-of-an-eye I found myself shoulder to shoulder with other cars ... all cruising along 85 north.

My Minneapolis sensibilities had failed me again. *Feces!* Those U-turns, another Atlanta invention, are express turnarounds for getting back on the freeway, not the frontage road. A tidal wave of misery engulfed me like a man-on-fire. I stepped on the gas persistent in the thought that tomorrow would be another day.

On the way back to Norcross, I did some mental cal-culations; 30 miles from Norcross to Alpharetta. 30 miles back. 20 miles from Norcross to downtown Atlanta and another 30 miles from there out to McDonough. Fi-nally, 65 miles from there back to Norcross when all the mistakes are added in. All told I had driven 175 miles.

I reflected on what I accomplished for my 175 miles. I bought a used camera, interviewed the owner's daugh-ters, again, experienced three distinguished traffic jams, got lost countless times, went in loops, and never got to see the movie I so desperately wanted to see. As a final footnote, my interview footage proved excellent.

# CHAPTER 5

The second the wheels of my car touched the pavement of the Martin Luther King Jr. National Historic Site I could feel the sanctity of the hallowed ground. I grew up in 1960s, and being a small tot, didn't have full appreciation for what was happening around me.

I didn't know Atlanta to be the epicenter of the Civil Rights Movement; I knew now. I gave deliberate thought to my decision to not interview anyone. Still pictures and silent video would have to do.

In 1968 our family took a trip to Washington D.C. We planned to drive through Chicago during the time they hosted the Democratic Convention. Race riots dominated the newspaper headlines, triggered by the assassination of Dr. King earlier that spring.

I remember the fear we felt approaching Chicago. My mom and dad discussed options in the front seat while us kids listened with tension from the back. Even as a tot I understood the whispered, anxious tones used by my parents. We drove right on thru.

Within days of the assassination of Dr. King our church held a special service to honor him. In the car on the way there I made a comment about Dr. King that as an ignorant eight year old I thought was funny, but my dad didn't see it that way. He isn't the kind to yell. But I remember his scolding lecture to this day, demanding I show respect and not accepting my ignorance.

It's really something special to have stood on the steps of the Lincoln Memorial in Washington D.C., the same steps Dr. King stood on when he delivered his *I Have a Dream* speech, and then years later stand on the steps of the National Historic Site that honors him.

A remarkable statue of Mahatma Gandhi stands on the walkway to Freedom Hall. Dr. King went to India for two months in 1959, the year I was born. He went to study the peaceful nonviolent ways of Gandhi. What he learned there became the hallmark of the Civil Rights Movement.

I had seen Gandhi's grave in New Delhi when I visited India over a decade ago. I remember having to take off my shoes. Visiting the grave had been a tourist sidebar. I said something to the cab driver to the effect of, "Isn't Gandhi's grave around here somewhere?"

"Yes, you want to go?" he asked.

"Where is it?"

"In Old Delhi," he replied, and we were off. We drove to the old part of New Delhi, on the west side of town, through colorful parks and brisk crowds. Ignorant, and arriving on the edge of history I didn't connect the dots.

To me it was just the gravesite of a famous spiritual leader who led the charge for India's independence; something they write about in high school textbooks. It was a tourist thing to do. I had to see it.

Standing today at Gandhi's statue near Freedom Hall and reflecting on Dr. King I felt a sobering void. Those two great men, Mahatma Ghandi and Dr. King, were forged together by history.

They shaped the world and they shaped me, but I've been too ignorant to know it. Only now can I connect the dots.

An abundant and colorful mural is painted along the length of a wall outside the front doors to Freedom Hall. Just by looking at it the epic struggle of Dr. King and his followers can be learned. In short, it's a precursor to the exhibits inside.

Walking through Freedom Hall is an instant replay of history. An entire culture launched a Movement to gain the basic rights set down in our Declaration of Independence, a document well over 200 years old. It says:

*We hold these truths to be self-evident, that all men are created equal, that they are endowed by their Creator with certain unalienable Rights, that among these are Life, Liberty, and the Pursuit of Happiness.*

As a society we've fallen short. We're in hiding and denial. The exhibits tell a morbid story, integrating strands to form a whole. In one exhibit, black and white photographs paint the injustices of the Jim Crow era for what they are. There is no good way to portray it.

The Civil Rights Movement is a tale of unsteady progress, where mountain tops were climbed and deep canyons fallen into. In one exhibit hangs a photograph of the famous march from Selma, Alabama, to Montgomery. The march is about, among other things, voting rights. If a picture says a 1000 words, this one says 2000. Above the marchers hangs a sign that reads, MONTGOMERY 34 MILES. Defeat is around the corner. But not one marcher is turning back.

In another, Dr. King is being booked at the police station, not a friendly face in the bunch. He's all alone in his tan suit and white fedora hat. He's an island unto himself. This photo symbolizes the stark obstacles he overcame to lead the Movement; death threats, bombings, scathing words, arrests, and physical aggression. He put himself out there at great personal risk. He didn't have to, but he did. *Courage.*

In its simplest form segregation is degrading. Part of the white strategy was to use "a time-tested system of psychological insults." Growing up in a nice little white suburb I don't pretend to understand. Photographs of signs that say FOR WHITE ONLY and NO COLORED PEOPLE ALLOWED IN ZOO TODAY put that ugliness on full display. In another photograph it declares COL-

ORED DINING ROOM IN REAR; the building is an out-house.

Lining the center of Freedom Hall are life-size wax figures of a blend of American Society: young, old, male, female, white, black, veteran, handicapped. In my mind it represents muted progress, but certainly not perfection.

A single room in Freedom Hall stands out for it's simplicity. It's lined with Jim Crow posters and is a microcosm of the Civil Rights struggle:

NO U.S. DOUGH TO HELP JIM CROW GROW
WE MARCH FOR INTEGRATED SCHOOLS NOW!
WE DEMAND EQUAL HOUSING NOW!
WE MARCH FOR JOBS FOR ALL NOW!
WE MARCH FOR VOTING RIGHTS NOW!
WE MARCH FOR EFFECTIVE CIVIL RIGHTS LAWS NOW!
WE MARCH FOR FIRST CLASS CITIZENSHIP

From those painful struggles came measured victories. Dr. King used the gift of the spoken word to initiate change. His *I Have a Dream* speech at the Lincoln Memorial on August 28, 1963, sticks out in most of our minds. It laid out a vision that America eventually accepted in fits and turns.

He finished with a flurry in his *I've Been to the Mountaintop* speech on April 3, 1968, at the Mason Temple in Memphis, Tennessee—the last speech he would ever give.

Dr. King's, *Letter from Birmingham Jail*, April 16, 1963 offered a stinging rebuke to those who said, *Wait*. In it he laid out his arguments that for 340 years the African-American nation has waited for their constitutional rights to be enacted. Rights that were handed down by God. Countries far and wide, he argues, are gaining their political independence, yet an African-

American in America can't sit at a counter in a restaurant and order a cup of coffee.

That same African-American suffers a litany of horribles at the hands of segregation: lynch mobs, cursing, insults, kicking, humiliation, and death. They experience endless poverty in a nation filled with affluence, yet that affluence is always just beyond their grasp. How do you explain to your children why they can't go to an amusement park advertised on TV or go to a play area because it is closed to colored children? How do you handle the tears? African-American parents see the change in their children: an inferiority forms and a hatred for whites emerges. How is an African-American supposed to live with the inner fears and outer resentments? Add it all up, Dr. King says, and we'll understand why he rejects those who say, *Wait.*

It's tragic that 50 years after voting rights were granted by the Civil Rights Act of 1965, they are being rescinded in some states. I won't try to understand the backward nature of this. What I do understand is that my eyes are opened. Freedom Hall is a celebration of truth. A painful truth, yes, but nonetheless a truth.

I ended my stay at Freedom Hall by walking past the exhibit containing the wooden carriage used to carry Dr. King's body at his funeral. It's ironic that both Gandhi and Dr. King led Movements based on nonviolence, created real change, but each went down through acts of violence. Those bullets ended their physical lives, but didn't slow down what both men started. The dots remain connected.

The new Ebenezer Baptist Church is a modern mega-structure right behind Freedom Hall. It's the living breathing aftermath of Dr. King, as modern and vibrant as ever. Across the street is the original Ebenezer Baptist Church, at the intersection of Auburn and Jackson. It's no longer an active church, but is a placeholder of history.

The rectangular blue sign with white letters hanging out front gives the original Ebenezer Baptist Church a small country church look, like I might find in the prairies of Minnesota or Iowa; brown brick with dual bell towers. But, it's in Georgia. Inside, it looks the same as those country churches. Brown pews, a pulpit, an area for the choir, and a balcony. Dr. King attended it as a child and served as its pastor as an adult. There at that pulpit, he delivered his fiery oration to the masses.

My emotions lagged behind my intellect. I got torn between the side of me that wanted be in somber reverence and respect, and the tourist side that wanted to tear through the place snapping pictures.

In the midst of this, a warm and hospitable black woman agreed to take my picture for me with my camera. Typical of the South, she went beyond a simple photograph, suggesting certain angles and certain pictures. It was her suggestion for me to stand next to a wall-sized black-and-white photograph of Dr. King, located in the stairwell between the first and second floors. This turned out to be one my best pictures of the afternoon. It's that Southern hospitality at work. It strikes when I least expect it, with results I can't comprehend, leaving my psyche as pleased as a Georgia Peach.

Next to the original Ebenezer Baptist Church are the white crypts where Dr. King and his wife, Coretta Scott King, are laid to rest side-by-side. Their crypts are in the middle of a long reflecting pool. I found myself standing and staring at the crypts for some time. In a strange way —it's hard to explain—it became the seminal moment of my entire trip.

President Lincoln and Dr. King existed a century apart, and both are icons. I learned about President Lincoln through history books, but Dr. King made his mark during my youth. A man who changed generations during my generation.

He led the Civil Rights Movement while being shot

at and people bombing his house; I played baseball and
football with my friends, and rode my bike and went to
movies theaters. I watched TV shows and learned the alphabet. I didn't experience the daily hand-to-hand com-
bat lived by the shakers and movers of this Movement. I
lived an insulated life. Perhaps it's that existence that
caused me to take a long pause in reflection for what Dr.
King and Coretta Scott King sacrificed. They lived it
while I only read about it, too young to know any better.

Near to the street is an eternal flame signifying Dr.
King's Spirit. It's no accident the skies burned blue and
the sun glistened bright. Dr. King affected us all whether
we want to admit it or not, some more than others. I
didn't fail to recognize this would most likely be the only
time I would ever visit there.

Speaking of Coretta Scott King, behind every great
man stands a great woman. She carried the torch after
him. On the far side of the reflecting pool, appropriately,
lies a building in her honor.

I left the grounds and strolled down the block to the
house where Dr. King grew up. My emotions didn't flow
as they did at the crypt or Freedom Hall. I had seen what
I came to see, to experience what I needed to experience.
The house was just a house.

I had one last destination of importance to me. I had
come to Atlanta to be a delegate for the National Education Association Representative Assembly. In a few days
I would be casting votes that would impact the children
and future of our country. I had to go see the school Dr.
King attended as a child.

The Dwight D. Howard Elementary school is only a
few short blocks from the Martin Luther King Jr. National Historic Site. I circled it by car, unable to tell if it
still functioned as a school or operated as some sort of
government office building.

The area around it felt uncertain. The building itself
looked run down with boarded up windows. Air condi-

tioners stuck out of a number of them, and a chain-link fence surrounded the unkempt grounds. I wondered if this is how it was when Dr. King went to school there.

Being it was mid-afternoon the time had come for another tourist destination, the Jimmy Carter Center. It should have been a straight shot there, but I managed to get lost. I found myself in the Old Fourth Ward. It's an old time neighborhood that's been transformed into a small, swanky entertainment district replete with swag. Buildings burst with the old rustic warehouse feel of yesteryear.

I walked along the sidewalk like a grubby tourist. I couldn't help but notice the yuppie couples, the kind that would live in those custom homes up in Alpharetta. They ate sophisticated omelets on glam dishware. The napkins they wiped their chins with were made of the finest materials, the silverware of the highest grade. Expense didn't appear to be an object of concern. Even the clear carafes holding orange juice made a statement. My rented Ford Fiesta parked among the Beamers on the street looked out of place.

Image is everything as the women were dressed to the nines, their men outfitted in regular jeans and tight fitting t-shirts. One gentleman added to the glam with neatly trimmed hockey scruff on his chin. The babes were impressed.

The restaurants were worldly, the menus exotic, developed by the finest chefs trained at the finest culinary schools. The dishes served ended up on the food network, with names the everyday man wouldn't be able to pronounce.

I walked on past the *clink* of the dishes, absorbing the aroma of the exotica and energized by the buzz in the air.

Sadly, all I could muster for myself was a frozen yogurt from the shop on the corner, a victim of a slim tight budget.

I asked for directions and proceeded to the Jimmy Carter Center a short distance away. Jimmy Carter was, by historical measures, a so-so president—perhaps too nice a guy for the job. He served during a time of rising interest rates, inflation, gas lines at the pump, and the Iran Hostage crisis.

During a debate with challenger Ronald Reagan he told the viewing audience how he had asked his daughter Amy what the biggest danger was in the world today. He said that she replied nuclear arms. I watched the debate live on TV. My first thought upon hearing that was, *stupid.* No 12 year old would have that on the top of their mind. Voters took notice, dooming Jimmy Carter to defeat.

Since being voted out of office he has shined on the world stage, putting the Carter Center on the map many times over. From brokering Mideast peace deals to an outspoken advocate for human rights he has earned his place in history as an honest man with a determined heart. It's for this reason I desired to visit. Besides, it's the tourist thing to do.

After arriving, I walked the grounds not sure what I would find. The parking lots were empty and the campus void. There are two main buildings. The Jimmy Carter Library and Museum, which by all accounts is a library and museum, and The Carter Center, where the nuts and bolts of what he does take place.

After parking I followed a curving footpath down some stairs to another curving footpath. I found The Carter Center, fronted by a small, but elegant reflecting pool. I was reasonably sure it was The Carter Center as it said CARTER PRESIDENTIAL CENTER in big chiseled letters on the front.

It was closed, which left only The Jimmy Carter Library and Museum to explore, but it wasn't obvious how to get there.

Meandering along, I couldn't help but notice the

Civil War history plaques dotting the sidewalks. I stopped to read the plaque about the Battle for Atlanta, immersing myself in the history of it all. After finishing, I hopped to the next one. And the next one. I followed this pattern for a bit before noticing an approaching security guard. I thought, *oh no*, he's gonna kick me out.

He didn't. Instead he engaged me in conversation about the logistics of the Carter Center. He let me know the library and museum were still open. They closed at 4:45 pm every day and it was now 4:30 pm. It would be better to come back another day when I had more time. This concluded my visit to the Jimmy Carter Center. I could scratch it off my bucket list.

So far in my life I've visited two Presidential Centers: The Harry S. Truman Presidential Library and the Jimmy Carter Center. In both cases I made it to the doorstep, but didn't go inside. It doesn't matter. The joy is in the journey.

# CHAPTER 6

I headed back across the freeway into the main part of downtown Atlanta, where Olympic Park sat. I hadn't been there since 1996 and I didn't know how I'd feel or what emotions would percolate or if I would feel anything at all. I can't deny my Olympic experience was a special period in my life.

When Pete and I left for the Olympics in 1996 we were both broke, not too different than today. On every trip certain events get etched in my memory with vivid clarity.

Back then Plymouth automobiles had kiosks in malls across the country. I worked at kiosks in the Minneapolis area setting up test drives. I was one of the best at this. To help pay for my Olympic experience I convinced my boss, who ran the program nationally, to let me also work a kiosk at a local Atlanta mall. She agreed wholeheartedly. I more than held my own.

Olympic Park was built specifically for the Olympics. So was Turner Field, which was converted for baseball after the Olympics, becoming the new home of the Atlanta Braves.

Downtown bustled with Olympic visitors. Not to repeat myself, but vendors hawked goods with abandon on every square inch of real estate. I still have an Olympic t-shirt I bought from one of them.

The three of us, Pete, Chris, and myself were trekking along Peachtree street jammed with Olympic tourists from every corner of the globe. Out of nowhere Chris, screamed "LOOK!" He pointed at something on the ground.

Lying there ready for nimble fingers to snatch was a wad of rolled up bills. We counted upwards of $4000. After a lively debate we made the decision to do the right thing and search for the owner. True Catholics. We asked around and found him, a German tourist. The wad had fallen out of his pants pocket.

We felt good about what we'd done. We could have kept the cash and who would know, but it was the right thing to do. Still true to this day.

Concerned for getting separated in the mass of humanity I implored Pete to set a meeting spot in case we got separated.

"No. No. We won't get separated," he said in smug confidence.

I front-loaded a great deal of sarcasm when I replied, "Okay." 45 minutes later I asked him, in all seriousness, "Where's Chris?"

"I don't know," he said, whirling his head in multiple directions. *Feces!*

We searched at a frantic pace as there wasn't a way for us to contact Chris. Back then cell phones weren't in vogue like they are today. Being he was 9 years old, this was a problem. We searched and searched. Blood pressures rose. Words spit like nails, Our feet pounded the pavement until raw. Emotions were near to erupting. But then, amongst the mania, we found him. After a scolding by Pete, a a soothing calm cast over us.

The Olympic spirit burned bright in Olympic Park. A stream of humanity rolled through it like a rustling river that never ends. The concerts, the events, the mass of tents, the flow of energy had no off switch. This uplifted our spirits well into the nighttime. But we left Olympic Park in a late night mad dash, screeching out of Atlanta and stomping on the pedal for an overnight drive to Miami. We didn't realize the soccer matches were at the Orange Bowl until a couple hours prior, when we finally took a look at the tickets. Crazy, I know.

Pete and I alternated driving. We high-tailed it non-stop to Savannah, Georgia, then made a sharp right, heading south along the ocean to St. Augustine, Florida. We stopped at a late-night gas convenience store so I could get money via Western Union. I wore my black backpack inside, tired and grubby. It's how I carried things.

"You better watch out for this guy," Pete smirked to the clerk, "he's shady. I'd check him out," pointing his finger with venomous motion at me.

The clerk glared at us for what seemed like minutes. "Do you know what happened?"

"No," we said in unison.

"A bomb went off at Olympic Park a couple of hours ago. It was in a backpack underneath a bench. A lady died and others were injured. They're looking for a white male." She went on to describe details as to where the bomb was placed, and a police description of the subject. For all I knew they could have easily been looking for me for the description she gave was similar in features to myself.

Pete's eyes opened wide, his mouth agape. "We were just in Olympic Park a few hours ago. We walked by that bench." We lost our smiles and scuttled the humor, departing in a somber mood for the rest of the long drive to Miami.

The bomber failed to dampen the Olympic spirit. I don't remember much of the soccer match itself between Brazil and Ghana though, but I do remember the flaming bright orange of the Orange Bowl seats and the manic soccer crowds, especially the Brazilians. They went bananas after their victory. Flags waved in force, dancing in the streets, chants, cheers. And somewhere in there, food. To this day we're still blown away by them.

My image of the Orange Bowl got formed watching the Miami Dolphins play football on TV. Don Shula, the coach, worked the sidelines always pacing back and forth. And when the Dolphins played it never failed to be a balmy sunny day. And the palm trees in the background always swayed in perfect harmony from the light breeze. It seemed so glamorous, so perfect on TV. I watched from the frozen tundra in Minnesota with envy. It's kind of strange, this is what I focused on during the soccer match. I loved the ambience of the palm trees, the crowds, the Olympic spirit, but tuned out the soccer match itself.

Back in Atlanta Pete had an extra ticket to the track meet at Turner Field. He sold it to a Mexican man for face value, $60. After he sold it we trampled into the stadium and up to our seats.

Midway through the track meet, a middle aged white gentleman sat down next to us, in the seat Pete had sold to the Mexican man. The gentleman had purchased it for $110, a nice profit for the scalper.

More interesting, he was a big time reporter for another major network. His network didn't own broadcast rights to this Olympics so he came as a fan. Pete recognized him and began a long conversation. I learned later he rose to fame due to his reports at previous Olympics. His next Olympic assignment was the Winter Olympics in Nagano, Japan, two years later. I still brag that we sat next to a big time Olympic reporter. Don't ask me for a name, for like a good politician, I don't remember.

Pete got left at a gas station in the middle of Wisconsin on the way back to Minnesota. The ensuing screams, a nonbeliever, a pay phone, and the Highway Patrol all combined to prove  these were *"the Greatest Olympics ever."*

\* \* \*

My reason for heading into downtown Atlanta, now, was to go learn about the world's most popular drink, Coca-Cola. On most trips I avoid tourist traps because they're just that. They seem too mamby pamby for me and I'd rather take the road less traveled. However, I just couldn't get around this one. Atlanta is home to the World Headquarters for Coca-Cola. It wouldn't matter if I wandered off the beaten path, I'd still end up sipping a Coke.

Reaching the outskirts of Olympic Park the dashboard clock read 5:07 pm. In a hurry, I pulled into the first parking lot I saw. A slim, squeaky clean, white suburban man approached, wearing a dark company polo shirt and reflective sunglasses.

The kind that says, *Look at me man, I'm cool.*

He asked, "Where are you going?"

I hadn't been paying attention and he caught me a little by surprise, "Oh, I'm going to the World of Coca-Cola. Do you know where it is?"

"I'll mark you down for 6:30 pm," he said, not so concerned with my question. "We have a Dave Chappelle show tonight right over there," he pointed to a building adjacent to the parking lot, "and we need this stall."

Taken aback, I said, "Well, I'm going to need a little more time. Make it 2 hours. If it's a problem for me to park here I can go elsewhere."

"No, that's ok. I'll mark you down for 7 pm. You look like a good guy. I'll only charge you $10. The World of Coca-Cola is right over there somewhere," pointing in the vicinity of Olympic Park. "I think it's on the other side of the park." He wasn't too good at hiding the fact that he didn't know, adding, "Hustle back. Don't be late. We need this stall."

"Ok," I said. As I walked along Olympic Park I realized that he had hustled me, and didn't care a hoot about me. His only concern was to fill a stall, and he got me to agree to a time limit so he could fill the stall with another person who'd pay more. This was wrong.

Just then I turned my head to the right and noticed a sign across the street, PARKING $3 ALL DAY. Salt in a wound. I burned to turn and yell, "You little no good *jerk!* Screw your stupid Dave Chappelle concert. You just jacked me for loose change. You *suck!*" He didn't even know where the World of Coca-Cola was, and he worked two blocks away. What a bum.

The World of Coca-Cola is right on the other side of Olympic Park. Not figuratively or sort of. It's like, right across the street. The beauty of staying at the Omni Hotel is that it, too, borders Olympic Park. Also, the Georgia World Congress Center, the Georgia Dome, and CNN Center are a stone's throw away.

I still remained skeptical of going to the World of Coca-Cola. I couldn't get over that it had the aura of band-aid populist tourism. That didn't seem to be a factor when I plopped my money down and bought a discount ticket good for both the World of Coca-Cola and CNN Center.

The lobby is impressive in its array of Coke Can art, where they have works of art in the shape of colorful Coke Cans using international themes. There are seven exhibits to see, each demonstrating a distinct aspect of Coca-Cola. The central foyer leading to these exhibits flows with bright fun colors courtesy of mural artists.

I performed a preliminary scan and scoped out my options. I narrowed my list of must see exhibits to three, maybe four, depending on how much time I had.

Moms and their hoards of kids lined up to get their pictures taken with the Coca-Cola Polar Bear. I lined up for a short while before exiting. It took up too much time on the clock. I hustled upstairs and gave cursory looks to other less desirable exhibits.

The Vault looked interesting. It looked more like it should be on the TV show CSI. The line to it snaked in horrible fashion and they only let in a certain number of people at any one time.

We entered an area illuminated by red lights, highlighted by a bank of whiz bang spymaster looking monitors. Hidden cameras projected our images up on the screens. This for sure gave it a CSI feel, which I have to admit, was pretty cool.

Exiting this area placed me in the part of The Vault that I can only describe as a history lover's dream. The hallways were stacked with goobs of touch and feel artifacts such as a yellow delivery truck and down-through-the-ages vintage Coca-Cola vending machines.

Coca-Cola is more than just brilliant at marketing. They're dynamic story tellers too. They tell their tale using plumb trivia facts and curious history.

All the while plastering splinters of old newspaper articles on the walls, bringing to life their fluctuating past. Central to the Coca-Cola story are the changes in ownership, the secret formula, and efforts to protect it. John Pemberton invented it. Asa Griggs Candler protected it. The Woodruff family grew it. And the company gone public blew it.

According to the Coca-Cola website, John Pemberton moved to Atlanta from Columbus, Georgia, in 1870, settling in a house on Marietta Street. It's there he concocted the first batch of Coca-Cola syrup in 1886. It went on sale for the first time at Jacobs Pharmacy, down the block from Pemberton's house, for 5 cents a glass as a fountain drink. Pemberton's partner and bookkeeper, Frank M. Robinson, penned the famous "Coca-Cola" trademark in an adaptation of Spencerian script.

There's a lot to learn in The Vault. During the first year sales averaged nine glasses a day. But then its popularity started to grow. Enter Asa Griggs Candler. In 1888 he started buying up all the rights to Coca-Cola. A slashing, savvy businessman himself, he propelled Coca-Cola to the next level.

The only person he trusted was himself, and fueled by this paranoia he built the Triangle Building on Edgewood Avenue. Inside, behind a fireproof door, he built the Triangular Room where he stored ingredients and mixed the formula together. He alone ordered the ingredients and locked away the purchasing records. Par for the course, he held the only key. He didn't stop there, inventing a way for others to produce the syrup without knowing what the ingredients were.

Asa Griggs Candler's own popularity paralleled that of the company he owned, being voted in as Mayor of Atlanta in 1916. He cashed in the chips in 1919, selling Coca-Cola to Atlanta banker Ernest Woodruff for $25 million.

Mr. Woodruff wasted no time taking the company public, issuing an IPO for 500,000 shares at $40 apiece.

Up until the time Ernest Woodruff purchased Coca-Cola from Asa Griggs Candler the formula had never been written down—by far the best way to protect it. Woodruff asked Candler's son to write down the formula and used it as collateral to secure a $25 million loan from Guaranty Bank of New York City. As part of the deal, he placed the document in the bank's vault. After paying back the loan in full in 1925, he moved the formula to the vault of Sun Company Trust in Atlanta.

Over the years, Coca-Cola learned to laugh and show us their flaws, like when they messed with the original formula in 1985 and the public screamed. It became the biggest debacle in their history. A couple of months after launching New Coke they canceled it, returning back to the original Classic Coke we all know and love so well.

Other stories painting their walls burst curious points of trivia. We learn how the distinctive Coke bottle got its shape. The questions over why Coca-Cola left India for two decades got answered. I couldn't pour through all of it for I existed in a time crunch.

As the popularity of Coca-Cola grew it soon found itself at the doorstep of history, possessing the most sought after trade secret in American History. Competitors came out of the woodwork, using every cloak and dagger scheme possible to score the formula. Imitators flooded the marketplace, selling fakes and palming off the Coca-Cola trademark. Coca-Cola fought back and won. No one could replicate the unique taste of the original, keeping the secret formula secure. One ad declares:

*IMITATIONS ARE MADE TO FOOL YOU, NOT TO PLEASE YOU, COCA-COLA IS BEING IMITATED AND WE OFFER $500 REWARD ... Don't allow an unscrupulous dealer to palm off on you something 'just as good.' ... Nothing is just as good as the original. We will take immediate legal steps to prevent such a fraudulent imposition upon the people.*

For deliberate reasons Coca-Cola doesn't have a patent for their secret formula. Instead, they choose to keep it a trade secret. Patents expire and at some point they would've had to share their secret formula with the world. They didn't want to.

By comparison a trade secret never expires, and they never have to tell anyone anything. The formula becomes a trade secret by the act of taking deep and verifiable security measures against a would-be thief. Their strategy works; it's been the most sought after trade secret in American history for the past 140 years.

Speaking of secrets, the most stunning discovery about The Vault exhibit is that the secret formula is stored in a real vault at the end of the exhibit. Not a fake, not an imitation. A *real* vault. It's in there, the secret formula, the thing John Pemberton created in 1886, just steps away from millions of visitors. Get too close and buzzers go off, alarms sound, red lights flare, and a voice warns to step away.

In 2011 Coca-Cola make the decision to move it from the Sun Company Trust vault to their own vault inside the World of Coca-Cola. This was not a random decision; they did so to coincide with an important date, their 125th anniversary. It stunned me they would be so bold as to place it in so public a place.

Next, I wandered through the in-house bottling plant. It's a real production line used to make the small bottles of Coke they give away at the end of the tour.

I came away in wonderment at the smooth efficiency and sophisticated science behind the simple task of putting soda in a bottle and slapping a cap on it.

The drive for science and sophistication came at the hand of Earnest Woodruff's son, Robert. By sheer persistence and force of will he raised the bar on the brand quality put into every bottle of Coke.

Each station is marked with a color coded circular sign identifying what that station is. For instance the *Water Treatment* station had a navy blue sign while the *Laser Coder* station had an orange sign. Putting so much thought and effort into each station made it more informative and fun for tourists like me to follow the steps in making a simple bottle of Coke.

After the last bottling station I cruised into the Taste Testing room. Coca-Cola makes different sodas and drinks for something like a bazillion countries around the world. This room offers an opportunity to sample some of those drinks.

For each drink, they identify what country it's sold in. For instance, *Thums Up* is sold in India while *Vegita-beta* is sold in Japan. *Lemon Crush* for Bahrain, *Beverly* for Italy, and *Smart* for China. *Bibo* for South America and South Africa, *Sparberry* for Zimbabwe, *Seagram's Ginger Ale* for Mozambique while *Stoney Tanawizi* stands tall in Tanzania ... and so on and so on.

When I was four-years old my grandma came over to chat with my mom. They were sitting at the kitchen table while I stood by a red hot burner on the stove. "Don't put your hand on that burner," my grandma said, "you'll burn yourself and it will hurt really bad." I believed her, but had to find out for myself. I plopped the full force of my hand on it. Within an instant I screamed bloody murder. The damage to my hand took weeks to heal.

As I neared my first Taste Testing station a nearby tourist said, "Don't try the Italy drink. It sucks. It tastes horrible and is the worst one in here."

My natural inclination was to believe him, but to try it anyways. I plopped my cup underneath the spigot and pushed the lever releasing the liquid. I brought the cup to my mouth and took a big swig. The bitter bite tasted like turpentine mixed with corn syrup. I started to spit it out simultaneous to my face contorting by reflex reaction.

"See what I told you?" the tourist said.

"You're right. That's terrible. How can anyone like that?" I asked, still spitting out the goo.

"I don't know man, I don't know."

The Italy *Beverly* drink casts a long shadow. Three months after arriving back in Minneapolis a co-worker and I had a meeting of the minds about the World of Coca-Cola. Six years earlier he had visited there too.

"Did you try the drinks in that one room?" he asked.

"The Taste Testing room? Yes, I did," I said.

"Did you try that one Italian drink? I remember it being the worst."

"Yes, I did. You're right, it was horrible. I don't know how anyone can stand it."

"I don't know either, but the Italians seem to like it," he said with an easy smile.

The time pressure I operated under forced a pause in my activities. I did some mental calculations and determined I could only stay a short time in the Taste Testing room. I'd have to pick up the pace and get moving. The parking lot attendant would be waiting and I had given my word. The forced efficiency I operated under paid dividends, though. In the end only the *Beverly* drink left my taste buds raw.

Coca-Cola never fails to take advantage of the opportunity to market themselves to visitors. Shepherded into a small movie theater, I sat and watched a short film about Coca-Cola that can best be described as dumb and dumber. It had a kid-corny mad scientist and an assistant spitting out door-knob vocabulary in annoying British accents. Fun though.

The dumb fun continued in the 4-D theater, playing a short, interactive movie about the secret formula; the seats move, water sprays, things poke, and best of all, it's all in 3-D.

Already convinced that the marketing people at Coca-Cola are geniuses, they cajoled me into a forced march to dispel any remaining doubts. I headed through a one-way turnstile down a hallway, with repeated warnings that this is a one-way ticket only.

I stuck my arm in the hole in the production display and grabbed my small, but free, bottle of Regular Coke, bottled a few floors above in that production line. After a few more tidbits are thrown in I'm shuffled to the end of the hallway where I moved my happy feet through an exit, receiving in return a pleasant smile and a "Thank you, have a nice day."

The one thing that strikes me as the twisted evolution of our modern world is that there are two kinds of Cokes: Regular and Mexican. Regular Coke uses high-fructose corn syrup and is predominately sold in the United States. Mexican Coke is manufactured in Mexico and contains real sugar. It's predominately sold in Central and South America, but is growing in popularity here.

Back in the good old days the Coke sold throughout the United States had real sugar, like today's Mexican Coke, but now it costs too much and we get the artificial stuff. In order to get the genuine Coke that used to be sold here, but that now isn't, we have to search the grocery aisles for Coke in a real glass bottle, and the check the label. If it says *hecho en Mexico*, bingo!

Somehow the logic doesn't fit, but I won't try to figure it out. To add insult to injury Mexican Coke has the label painted on, like the original back in the day, whereas with Regular Coke we get plastic bottles with the label glued on. And now for the genius part.

After gliding through the exit I found myself in the middle of their big, outsized, colorful, gleaming souvenir store replete with super friendly helpful staff and gobs of every kind of souvenir imaginable. I don't know if they borrow this strategy from Las Vegas casinos or if they invented it.

It isn't a matter of wondering if they have what I want, it's a matter of understanding that whatever I want is there, for a price. My cheap, slim-tight budget demanded I stick to one low-cost t-shirt; no other souvenir allowed.

But which one? I narrowed it down to one artsy t-shirt. I cruised to the cash register to thwart any weakness, but fussed and fidgeted along the way, suffering the throes of indecision. I experienced apprehension, for the hour had come to fork over my parking stall. Seconds away from the cash register I ditched the artsy low cost t-shirt, choosing instead a plain, but catchy, black t-shirt with I HAD A COKE IN ATLANA imprinted above a Coke logo, for more money.

Those geniuses sitting in their ivory tower a few blocks away giggled, knowing they had a sucker in their grasp; I snatched a simple red Coke mug too, closing out my visit to the World of Coca-Cola. The clerk handled me with another purifying dose of Southern hospitality, which they seemed to know I love so much.

What I really did that day was pay Coca-Cola for the right to enter their museum, so I could buy an advertisement on a t-shirt that I would wear for free, for years, promoting them. And don't forget the mug. Las Vegas, here I come.

\* \* \*

I'm wired like a true Catholic. Having primary concern

for the happiness of the parking lot attendant, I whisked through the doors of Coca-Cola to the outside world and made a bee-line back to the lot.

I worked up a sweat and kept my feet moving. It didn't matter that I was the tourist spending money and buying souvenirs and pumping up the local economy. I had an attendant to please.

I arrived back at my car out of breath and only a minute or two past 7 pm. The attendant, an employee of National Parking Solutions, asked with curious friendliness, "How'd you like it?"

"Fun," I replied. "Hey, do you know where Fox Bros. Barb-B-Q is?" I had innocent faith he would know.

He didn't receive my question with discernible concern, barely giving a cursory glance. "Don't have a Smartphone, huh?" he said, turning and walking towards the street. "I have to go wave my flag and get cars in here."

"I'll follow you. I can wait."

Out in the street he made a veiled attempt to help, punching a button or two on his Smartphone before quitting and going back to waving his red flag. He interjected, "I can't help you now. If you want to wait a few minutes ...."

"Forget it," I said, not feeling it. First I have to hustle, and now I have to wait.

# CHAPTER 7

The time had come to move to my true secondary purpose in Atlanta. Barbeque. Fox Bros. Bar-B-Q lay in my sights. They were consistently rated high in my internet searches, so I chose them over Fat Matt's and Heirloom. I knew they weren't very far away, but I didn't know how to get there. I called them for directions, but the girl answering the phone couldn't help.

I began a journey of discovery for WiFi. I found a Barnes & Noble, but they had closed at 6 pm. I drove all over the campus of Georgia Tech on the edge of downtown and met defeat. Somewhere in there my cell phone ran out of power. I looped back to the area near Underground Atlanta and struck out again, driving in aimless directions and gaining in desperation.

By accident I came across Midtown Tavern. I found a workable solution, with free parking on Sundays, WiFi, open tables, and a chance to charge up my cell phone. I ordered a Diet Coke and fired up my laptop, gaining the directions I desired.

Sitting at the bar in front of me was a swanky, twentysomething couple. The strikingly beautiful woman had long flowing black hair, and wore chic, cosmopolitan glasses. The man, slim and chic himself, had a generous repose of hockey scruff, and took long puffs on a cigarette. Not like a sailor at a bar. No. Long sophisticated drags followed by a tilt of the head upwards and slow sexy exhales.

He handed the cigarette to the woman, who proceeded to take her own long sophisticated drags. She, too, did a tilt of the head upwards and made slow sexy exhales. I watched this with indignation.

This glam couple acted super cool with their long drags and smooth exhales, taking it to a new art form. But they were idiots. All they were doing was turning their lungs black and polluting the world. I found it quite silly, if not outright stupid.

I sauntered up to the bar and asked the bartender, "How much for the Coke?"

"Don't worry about it," he said.

I felt an explosion of warmth. A kind soul uttering four little words restored my faith in Southern hospitality. They say that if a customer has a good experience, they tell ten people, but if they have a bad experience they tell twenty.

I'm here to dispel that. I had a good experience at the Midtown Tavern in southeast downtown Atlanta and I want to tell the entire world—all six billion of you. Go there and be happy. You'll leave with a wonderful experience.

Even with directions in hand, getting to Fox Bros. proved to be a bigger challenge than I imagined. I doubted the logic of the directions, believing I must have missed a turn or two. What threw me, to borrow a few words from Robert Frost, is that "two roads diverged in a wood, and I, I took the one less traveled by." If I took a left it's Braircliff/Moreland, and if I took a right it's Dekalb. I took the right onto Dekalb and a few blocks down took another right onto Dekalb. *Wait a minute.*

My directions gave the illusion of a misprint, *take a right on Dekalb* followed by *take a right on Dekalb,* but the physical reality is I took a right on Dekalb, and then another right on Dekalb. It all made sense when I did as told and curved up over the bridge to find Fox Bros. Bar-B-Q waiting for me.

They are big and bright, full of action, the small parking lot squished with cars. The glowing neon sign at the top of the building lit up the night sky and erased all doubt.

The Fox Bros. name stenciled in white letters in the shape of a circle on the red building looked like a cowboy had gone crazy with a branding iron.

There's a large outdoor area where white Christmas lights hang from the beams, making it more than possible for the patrons to eat there. Walking inside, the atmosphere had elements of the old west. Not a traditional saloon feel, but urban honky tonk. The memorabilia splattering the walls, the music pouring from the speakers, the wooden tables, the groove and jibe, the darker lighting, all honky tonk.

I grabbed a round table. Business boomed with waiters and waitresses moving quick. The buzz and churn of the patrons electrified the air, and the smell of sweet barbeque added a charm and hue to the nighttime.

A waitress arrived ready to take my order. She looked to be white suburban and of college age. I pestered her, "Are you camera shy? I like to eat barbeque when I visit new places and I interview people wherever I go to post them on YouTube. I'm writing a travelogue book about everything too. Can I interview you?"

In a strange sort of way, asking her for an interview was akin to asking her for a date. There's a pause and tension in the air before the answer arrives. "Let me think about it. I'll let you know," she said. This sounded familiar.

I was quite hungry so I shrugged it off and placed my order, "I'll have the baby back ribs and baked beans. By-the-way which do you like better, the potato salad or coleslaw?"

"I'd go with the potato salad." And so I did, with a Diet Coke to boot.

I pestered another waitress for an interview, "Excuse me, I like to interview people wherever I go. Are you camera shy?"

"Big time," she said, scooting along.

I continued my pestering, asking the waitress who brought my order, "Can I interview you?"

"Not a chance."

My plate came with tater tots, an unexpected thrill. In the first grade my mom volunteered at the school cafeteria, and the best days of my first grade career were when she worked and they served tater tots.

Now for the play-by-play: the ribs were authentic. The sauce was sweet, but not over the top. The potato salad had a made-by-mom quality; nice and gooey, something I would expect for a place of this caliber. The baked beans were an urban fusion of an old country recipe.

But let's talk tater tots. Gosh darn they were good. With every bite the memories of first grade came to life. Fox Bros. kept it simple; put them on a pan and heat them.

The great thing about tater tots is they melt in your mouth. With each bite I could feel the little particles of potato scrub against the roof of my mouth. I loved it because they tickled my throat, too, as they slithered on down.

Something about the ribs didn't add up. They were similar in texture to Arthur Bryant's in Kansas City, which is saying a lot. The meat came off the bones in a similar way. No, that isn't what's strange. Smokey too. Unlike Arthur Bryant's the sauce had a sweet twinge to it, but no that wasn't it either.

"Geez, these ribs are huge," I said, figuring it out. I dare say succulent. Thick too. Baby back ribs are supposed to be smaller. These filled out the plate. I waited for the waitress to come back so I could warn her that a mistake had been made.

Too focused on pestering her, I soon forgot, asking instead, "Have you thought about letting me interview you?" I'm nothing if not persistent.

"I'm still thinking about it. I'm talking to others."

I went back to doing damage to those ribs, chomping down with ease. In between bites I observed the waitress talking to another employee, a white male wearing a red Fox Bros. T-shirt.

He walked over, shook my hand and introduced himself, "Hi, I'm Scott."

"Are you camera shy?"

"Hell no. I'm the manager." I pulled out my camera and we began.

I said, "You know, these baby ribs sure are big for baby back ribs. I was beginning to wonder if they were rack ribs. They sure are big."

Scott explained. "We only have one store and we are the number one seller of ribs in *all* of Georgia. Therefore we get our first pick of ribs. We don't get the small ones, we get the big ones that fill the plate," holding his hands far apart.

If I looked up the word resilient in the dictionary, I'm sure I would find a picture of Fox Bros. next to it. Scott told me a story, "Presidents Wood, our neighbors, gave us a live tree for our five-year anniversary and it fell on us during a big storm. It wiped out the dining room, the area next to us. We have two catering vans, one that's twelve years old and a newer one with 300 miles on it. Of course the tree crushed the newer one." He showed me pictures. That big hog of a tree crushed it flat as a pancake, like when a car goes through the crusher in a scrap yard.

"We re-opened within 36 hours," Scott continued, "We erected a big tent and operated out of there. When we took down the tent to rebuild the outside dining area we closed for only four days. We re-opened on Memorial Day."

"Wow, most businesses wouldn't do that."

"Most businesses couldn't. We wanted to be aggressive. We didn't want to sit and collect insurance money like others. We could have walked away.

But we wanted to stay loyal to our employees. We sent a message to our customers we are here to stay." Fox Bros. is like the postman; neither rain nor sleet nor snow nor big nasty tree will stop them.

I soaked this in and pondered—*36 hours*—unheard of.

"Do you want to see our smokers out back?" he asked.

"Yes," I said, trying to contain myself. I hit the ON button to start rolling the video. Conveniently, the camera ran out of power. From here on out it would have to be the power of visualization for me.

During the tour, Scott pointed to a big black smoker, "In the beginning we used this big black can. We call it a manual. It has a temperature gauge, but no way to regulate the temperature."

It looked menacing. It's what I visualize when I think of barbeque in the classic sense of the guy on the street corner smoking ribs with aroma filling the neighborhood. It's basically a 55 gallon drum sawed in half.

"As business grew we couldn't keep up. It took too long. We transitioned over to these Southern Pride commercial smokers." It took a bit for it to register that Southern Pride is a brand name. "We only use the manual can for special events," Scott continued. "When you come back, you have to try the chicken wings. They're our specialty. They're huge," he held his hands far apart. "They're out of this world. You have to try them."

Various sized Southern Pride smokers jammed their kitchen. Most stuff is cooked anywhere between 200-230 degrees. Contrary to popular belief commercial smokers don't use gas to cook the meat. They operate like a manual can, but with a twist. The natural gas used in the commercial smokers heats the wood, and it's the heated wood, like in a manual can, that cooks the meat.

The commercial smoker has the ability to regulate heat automatically without human intervention. That's a major benefit over a can. That combined with the ability to rotate the meat automatically churns out a higher quality, more uniformly cooked meat, but keeps it authentic.

He kept referring to one smoker as an 800 pounder and another as a 1000 pounder. Confused, I asked, "What does 800 pounder or 1000 pounder mean?"

"Smokers are rated by poundage. For example, let's say a pork butt weighs 10 pounds. If you do the math, a smoker that's a 1000 pounder can cook 100 of them at once. The higher the poundage the more it can cook at once."

"Interesting. What's the story behind Fox Bros.? How did it start?"

Scott, blessed with a gift for storytelling, began. "The Fox brothers are originally from Texas. They came to Atlanta for corporate jobs and started hosting backyard parties. They served barbeque and had bands and everything. These were huge successes. They were just doing it for fun, but also they won awards from Atlanta newspapers and they hadn't entered any contests. A local bar got wind of them and asked them to cook barbeque for them on Wednesdays. This took off and soon the bar asked them to cook every day of the week."

Scott's voice rose a little, the words spilling out at an increased velocity, and his eyes opened wider. "Eventually the bar just handed out the Fox Bros. menu instead of their own. It so happened one of the Fox brothers got laid off from his corporate job.

They all looked at each other and decided to join forces. The bar owners knew business and the Fox brothers knew barbeque. From that day on, Fox Bros. Bar-B-Q was born. We've been open for six years, have only one store, and one sauce too."

I paused for a second or two, absorbing all this.

"Starting a business is no small task. I started one once and flopped miserably." I had awe for what I heard.

Scott continued, "The building in its original form, the part we're sitting in, used to be an old Texaco gas station. A picture of that station is over there on the wall," pointing to a picture behind him near the kitchen door.

I got up and walked over and took a look. It looked like a gas station I might see in the 1950s.

"To keep that old feel, when we rebuilt after the tree fell, we added garage doors, which you can see above us," now pointing above. I tilted my head skyward and saw them. "One nice thing is we can open and close them based on the elements."

"Interesting. It's booming in here tonight, on a Sunday. Is it always booming like this?"

"This is slow."

"Slow? Are you kidding me? *Slow?*" I didn't believe him. "Yes, from Father's day to Fourth of July is our slow time. Come back on the Fourth of July, we'll be booming!"

With every person I interview, I walk away with some trivia the camera doesn't catch. In Scott's case he has college connections to friends in Memphis, Tennessee.

Some of those friends know Fred Smith's son. They party with Fred Smith's son in Fred Smith's house, which is a mansion befitting a king.

For those who don't know, Fred Smith started Fed Ex. He's rich. Very rich. According to snopes.com, Fred Smith presented his idea for Fed Ex as a paper for a class assignment in college.

Urban Legend has it that his professor told him the idea was dumb and dumber, it would never work, and gave him a bad grade. This part of the story seems to be more myth than truth. Fred Smith himself doesn't recall what he got on that paper.

Any businessman will tell you that a key to business success frequently comes down to three words: location, location, and location.

Scott explained, "Dekalb runs straight from downtown Atlanta to Decatur, and we're in the middle. Atlanta and Decatur are the two largest cities in Georgia. Business people like us because we're a straight shot no matter what direction they come from. Also, we're on top of the bridge, easy to find. Others have tried and failed here, but they were located under the bridge."

The time had come to depart, and I said my good-byes. "Don't forget," Scott said, "when you come back get the chicken wings. They're huge and they're awesome."

I took Dekalb straight into downtown Atlanta ready to enter 85 north for the trek to Norcross. I got lost again and made curious loops to nowhere. I drove along a side street bordering the freeway and came to a stop at an intersection.

As I waited for the light to turn green, I turned my head to the right and saw the shadow of a building hiding on the corner. It looked worn and bruised from decades of existence, a hole-in-the-wall if I ever saw one. It's color, a dim faded red. The sign read CLOSED, but I made out the name on top of the building (note to self ... *Thelma's Kitchen*).

# CHAPTER 8

On Monday morning my alarm went off at 6:30 am, but I didn't get up right away which led to a mad dash later. I had time for one more Super Salad before packing my stuff for the haul to the Omni Hotel in downtown. I had the brilliant idea to bring my left over food with me to the Omni, even though I'd be on someone else's dime.

I took numerous trips between my room and car, packing it with who knows what. It's amazing how much I had accumulated in just a few days. I headed south on 85, skipping Planet Fitness, and getting nervous.

I had to return my Hertz rental car by 11 am. As I drove doubts crept in as to whether I had the car registration materials with me, thinking I might have left them back at the motel. I stopped to check and breathed a sigh of relief when I found them.

I struggled finding my way back to the freeway, driving in chaotic loops around downtown. Little beads of sweat formed on my forehead as I calculated the late fees Hertz might charge as it looked more doubtful I would get the car back to them on time. The pressure of operating on a slim-tight budget never eases. This cruel menace finds a way to rob joy at every opportunity.

After loops to nowhere I found the freeway and trekked onward. I found the airport exit and zoomed along the curvy road like I did at LAX in Los Angeles. I hurled a curse word or two after seeing 11:27 am on the car clock. *Fees!*

I found nothing but courteous friendly faces when I pulled into the Hertz check-in area. "Don't worry about anything, we'll take care of it," the attendant said.

"Thank you," I said with a glow as I hopped out of the car.

"Have a great day sir!" she said, with a big Hertz smile.

"You too!"

* * *

The interaction between cab driver and cab rider, many times, is an exercise in International Relations bolted to Negotiations 101. My cab driver originated from Eritrea, a small East African country bordering the Red Sea. It sits right on top of Ethiopia and Somalia. He couldn't have been more friendly, chatting up stuff about Atlanta, Turner Field, the weather, and curious about Minneapolis.

I played up I was a delegate for the NEA convention. "Lot's of educators flocking to Atlanta," I told him.

He liked that. More prospects for business. I meant to ask him about Eritrea, but found it more interesting that Atlanta is considering putting a retractable roof on Turner Field. I lamented the misery of the Dome in Minneapolis and cheered over the new Vikings Stadium. He didn't escape my stories of the 1996 Olympics; he seemed genuinely impressed.

I made two mistakes during the short ride to the Omni Hotel. First, I hinted at the possibility of needing a rental car again later in the week. This got translated into: "I take you to Omni. You drop off things. I take you back to airport for car." I could see the $$ signs in his eyes.

"No, no, no," I said. "I don't need the car now, but maybe later in the week. You can just drop me off at the Omni, that will be good enough. I have no where to park it." Round one for me.

Second, I bragged repeatedly that my union is paying for the trip.

A smile broadened his face, "You give me big tip! Extra tip! Your company pay! Big tip!"

"Ok, you got me on that one. I'll give you an extra big tip." Round two for him. Arriving at the Omni, I honored my word.

I followed the escalators up to the main floor and navigated the hallways, finally arriving at the front desk ready to plow through the check-in process. I started in with, "The last time I was in Atlanta was for the 1996 Olympics ...." The clerk, chatty and helpful, took pleasure in that like so many others before her.

Standing there while she punched some buttons on her computer screen I felt the toll of persistent sinus troubles and a general lack of sleep. I ached from the weight of my backpack.

The annoying clutter of holding multiple bags full of stuff from the motel didn't make it any easier. If I was going to save pennies by taking everything with me, I was going to do it big.

"Do you have a credit card?" she asked.

"Why do you need a credit card? In case I order extras?"

"No sir, it's to pay for the room."

"There must be a mistake. My room is prepaid by my union. I verified it back in Minneapolis."

She punched a few more buttons on her screen, "No, sir, it's not. I'll need your credit card."

I had the beginnings of a heart attack. I was at a point where I could focus on nothing else but dropping my stuff in the room and plopping on the bed for a warm, restorative nap. Fatigue had taken its pound of flesh. Doom descended. Staggering from this sudden blow, in a blink, I became a man without a room.

I *know* back in Minneapolis I asked someone from the union if they prepaid the room, and the answer came back yes. The wiring in my brain might be mixed up, but not that mixed up. I knew what I heard.

My credit card only had enough space on it for auxiliary trip expenses and the rental car. It did not have space for a $1000 room charge. Such is the life of an Education Assistant. I'm nothing if not persistent, and thinking on my feet has saved me many times before.

I forged an option where I'd bag the room and go rent a car, again, from the downtown Hertz office a few blocks away. I would drive back to Norcross, reclaim my motel room, and commute every day. I could park in downtown for only $3 per day. That I could prove.

But I had convinced myself I had to check-in for the Assembly by a certain time. The constant pressure of always having to be somewhere is annoying. It robs the fun. I left the front desk and searched out the Education Minnesota check-in table upstairs.

Upon finding them I set my backpack and bags down on the floor and began to spill my tale. "I went to check-in downstairs and they said I needed a credit card to pay for the room. I swear I asked someone from the union before I left if they prepay the room and they said yes. I don't have $1000 available on my credit card. I'm an Education Assistant and I'm at the bottom of the totem pole. I have all my stuff with, I'm tired, I want to take a nap. Now I'm going to have to rent a car, drive back to where I came from in Norcross, and drive every day."

Rita, from Education Minnesota, listened to my ramblings with the grace of an Angel, delivering a soothing calm I had been so lacking. In a mom sort of way she took control.

State delegates have their rooms prepaid by Education Minnesota, she explained, while in the case of local union delegates it is up to the union how they do it. Each one is different.

She offered up a plan. If I could get a hold of our union president, and he gives her the go ahead, she would bill my room to Education Minnesota and the union can reimburse them later. I hustled off downstairs to the coffee shop.

I made a flurry of phone calls, leaving tense voice-mails, and typing frantic messages to every email address I thought would matter. Full of desperation I scurried back upstairs to Education Minnesota. By now my sleep deprivation had reached a maximum, my blood pressure was at new highs, and my nerves were thoroughly shot.

Rita worked her magic and put me at ease, reassuring me this happens every year, saying, "please don't worry about it."

When I work with students I'm supposed to be the calm one, the one modeling behavior. Now, the tables had turned. I was the anxious one, the angry one, the brat.

I scurried back down to the coffee shop, scouring every new email in my inbox, looking for that go ahead from the union president. Not finding the success I was looking for I bolted back up to Rita.

She had good news. "I talked to your union president, and everything is taken care of." Beautiful.

Once in the room I threw my crap on the floor with a thud and dove headfirst into the warm comfy bed. I had dodged a bullet. I still wondered how I could have heard so wrong back in Minnesota. I mentally implored our union to change their policy. Making someone on the low end of the totem pole fork out $1000 bucks upfront is a killer on the stress. With that I fell asleep.

After my nap I headed downstairs to the conference room housing our state caucus. I learned about Representative Assembly (RA) protocols. The RA is where the National Education Association (NEA) takes care of all its national business.

Each state or caucus sends delegates who vote on NEA constitutional amendments, standing amendments, legislative policies, and new business items that affect education at all levels throughout our land. What we do here impacts, literally, every child in America.

In our state caucus meetings the leadership rolls

through each agenda item for the day. Caucus committees study these items in advance and make recommendations to the larger caucus whether to vote for or against a particular item.

We debate the issue on the caucus floor, and then vote, taking an official non-binding caucus position. In the main Representative Assembly I'm allowed to vote the way I see fit and I'm under no obligation to vote according to the official Minnesota Caucus position.

The next morning I slugged it over to the Georgia World Congress Center (GWCC) and headed straight to the exhibit hall. I engaged delegates from Alabama in a discourse on barbeque in Atlanta. If anyone knows a thing or two about barbeque, they do. They had scoped out downtown, tried some, and burned for more. I drooled for an opportunity to hook up with them in the days to come.

Vendors in the exhibit hall hawked everything from gourmet peanut butter to African clothing. Very few exhibits had a direct connection to education. That's what made it interesting; the people, life, and schmoozing. I filled my groaning backpack with an abundance of free stuff.

Feeling the need to participate in more serious delegate business, I popped into the Budget Committee meeting in the main Assembly Hall. Stepping through the black curtains the immensity of it took on the texture of a rock concert. Back in the day I use to work as an usher for rock concerts at Met Center in Bloomington, Minnesota, so I would know.

The sparse crowd of delegates in attendance looked like ants amongst the throngs of black empty seats. The Committee poured through spreadsheets and charts and numbers, reams of them. Boring, but necessary. The sheer size of the main stage had the ability to intimidate the everyday man.

Red, white, and blue rocket size banners hung along

the back wall. I walked to a center aisle and stopped, rotating 360 degrees as I soaked it all in. It's all I could do.

I decided to pop into the Constitution, Bylaws, and Standing Rules meeting held in a small hallway conference room. We had been encouraged by caucus leadership to attend some of these meetings to get our feet wet.

Inside the conference room delegates discussed, debated, and dissected proposed Constitutional amendments, By-Laws, and Standing Rules to be discussed, debated, and dissected at the main Representative Assembly.

Like the NFL preseason, things are tried out and evaluated. NEA President Van Roekel led the session. A former high school math teacher, he was impressive in his ability to command an audience, manage the discussion, wither criticism, and shut down debate if it turned ugly; skills honed by his years in the classroom.

Lunch Time! I headed across the street to Taco Mac. Nestled on the street side of CNN Center, it bustled with lunchtime customers. I placed an order for a Taco Combination Platter and waited.

I struck up a conversation with a twentysomething gentleman with tattoos down his arms. He waited for his order too. We got talking barbeque and he told me of his favorite place called *This Is It!*, on the southwestern edge of Atlanta. It's a place I already had high on my list, but logistics had prevented me from going there. His knowledge of barbeque isn't what made him interesting. It's his fanaticism about soccer.

He's a walking billboard for the sport. I used to think my friends from Peru were the world's biggest soccer fanatics, but he put them to shame. To say he eats, breath, and sleeps soccer would do a grave injustice. He's much more than that. He plays, coaches, cheers, and jeers every soccer tournament he can get to.

And it doesn't matter where the game is played. When I asked him if I could interview him he replied with an emphatic, "*NO!*" Concerns about being seen by work, he said.

More interesting, he would be attending a big soccer tournament in Minnesota in a month. He didn't know where, he only knew he was going. It had to be the National Sports Center in Blaine, Minnesota. It's where all the big soccer tournaments in Minnesota are held. We all have something that's in our wheelhouse, and for him, it's soccer.

Fresh off my conversation I realized I'd been waiting a long time for my Taco Combination, and that others who came after me had gotten theirs first, including the soccer guy. Always the patient one, I inquired with the bartender. He went and checked and came back with bad news, they screwed up my order.

"Just a few more minutes," he pleaded.

"I'm sorry, I have to get back. Could you cancel it please? It's alright, not a worry."

The fire in his eyes told me he rejected my people pleasing, that's ok, no worries attitude. Mine wasn't the only order screwed up. Pissed at the kitchen staff, he let loose with a, "That's bull!" As I headed out the door I refused to look back, out of fear I'd witness him strangling a cook.

Still hungry, I headed over to Olympic Park to grab a hotdog and fries from their concession stand. Not the same as a Taco Combination, but it would do. On my way back I cut through the hotel and bugged the concierge about the best barbeque in Atlanta.

She rattled off a few, but went for the gold in naming Bone Lick BBQ her favorite. I queried her some more, but she stuck with her original choice. She said, "I like the others, they're good, but I like Bone Lick the best. I'd go there."

She whipped out a promotional postcard from behind the counter and thrust it towards me. I whisked it from her grasp, and slung it into my backpack. Persuaded, I made a split second decision that this is where Rinker and I would go.

Heading back to the GWCC a thought occurred that my numerous treks to and from the Assembly Hall in the course of a day constituted a legitimate workout. By the numbers the GWCC is 3.9 million square feet (gwcc.com), and organized into three buildings, A, B, and C. By comparison, the Minneapolis Convention Center is only 1.6 million square feet (minneapolis.org).

Getting down and dirty, the Minneapolis Metrodome is a paltry 415,000 square feet (geom.uiuc.edu), and 9.375 of them would fit in the GWCC. That's a lot of real estate. To add fuel to the fire the Assembly Hall is on the far end of Building B, meaning I had to walk virtually the entire length of the thing to get to or from my seat on every single trek.

* * *

In the Representative Assembly all decisions are ultimately made by the delegates. Take for example New Business Item 25. It reads:

*The National Education Association will work with the U.S. Department of Education to encourage the individual states to designate physical education as a mandatory subject.*

When it came up the moderator on stage read it to the Assembly. Those delegates wishing to speak went to the microphone closest to them and handed the assistant working the mic their request slip. Then they waited.

The assistant working the mic then phoned in the delegate's request to the stage, dictating the information on the slip to the person answering the phone. Those people in turn wrote everything down on their own slips, and handed them to the moderator, who in turn called delegates to the mic in the order of slips received. This process was not too different than a roll of the dice.

The Representative Assembly is a political convention in its simplest form. The political heavy hitters were out in force, coalitions formed, and gamesmanship was the norm. One of the dirty tricks is that when a delegate is called to speak he or she could pass their time to another microphone.

A strategy was enacted to take competitive advantage of this loophole, where a coalition worked in concert with others to get a specific delegate to the microphone who was a persuasively blessed public speaker. In other words, they got their home run hitter to the plate.

The moderator got to decide whether to let all speakers talk or if enough was enough and it was time to vote. Usually the moderator was President Van Roekel. Delegates had three minutes to speak and he was brutal in cutting them off when they went over.

One of the things I always preach to students in my communications class is that humans have a very very short attention span. You may be the best speaker in the world, but if you go on too long you will lose your audience and they won't hear a word you say.

As a junior at the University of Minnesota I had to take *Fundamentals of Oral Communication*. To this day it remains my favorite class. I had a strong A-grade going into the Final, and I had 8 minutes for my Final speech.

A lot rested on it. Normally I prepped by practicing many times over in the days leading up to the big moment. I would bring an alarm clock and set it for the time limit allowed, and then practice, practice, practice.

For that Final I didn't prepare like I normally do and I didn't practice. When I gave my Final speech the instructor cut me off at 13 minutes. I received a B-grade for the class; lesson learned.

Delegates fire up their passions when they get to the mic. Some are more gifted than others. Some items are hotly debated with gut-felt raw emotions while others are mere mop-up operations. The one thing I've learned about educators is they don't hold back. They have opinions and by golly we're going to hear them.

After President Van Roekel closes the debate for an item, a show of hands is made; that's how we the delegates vote, with our hands. If he's unsure of the outcome then he takes another vote saying, "Those in favor say YES." He waits for the screams to die down, then implores, "those against say NO."

Usually he and his stage hands could determine the outcome based on the verbal vote. However, if a delegate didn't like the outcome he or she wielded great power in challenging it. Only one delegate need yell "Division," and we were on.

Division is a pronounced visual vote. "All in favor stand," President Van Roekel declares. Those delegates stand. He and his stage hands make an estimate. Those delegates sit. "All against stand," he declares. Those delegates stand. He and his stage hands make an estimate. Those delegates sit.

After a final confer with his stage hands President Van Roekel announces to the Assembly whether the item had passed or failed in the Division vote. The item is settled ... unless someone yelled "Roll Call." It takes only one delegate to yell this to start that process.

Roll Call is the most granular and numerically accurate of all the vote counting methods. The most painful, rigid, and time-consuming one too. A vote is first taken to decide if we the delegates even agree to initiate a Roll Call.

And if a two-thirds majority of us agree, then we're on. "Don't be stuck outside during a Roll Call," our Minnesota Caucus leadership warned us on day one.

During a Roll Call no one is allowed in or out of the Assembly Hall during the count. If I'm in the bathroom when it happens I'm not allowed back in. I can't vote. My voice isn't heard. I'm out of luck.

In a Roll Call each individual caucus polls their delegates and tallies them. The results are submitted to the stage where the bean counters add them up. There are 11,000 delegates in the Assembly Hall and it takes time, perhaps hours, to do the bean counting. Once all the votes are counted, all 11,000 of them, the results are announced. *Don't be stuck outside the Hall during a Roll Call.* I won't I told myself that first day.

Certain topics at the Representative Assembly touched a few nerves and set off a firestorm. The topics of sexual orientation and same-sex marriage did far more than that. It engulfed the entire Assembly.

One delegate, a black man from the South, unloaded. He objected on "Christian grounds" against a by-law that would incorporate a more liberal interpretation of sexual orientation in classroom lessons. "It goes against my Christian beliefs and I cannot and will not do it," he said, his decibel altering words exploding from the speakers, adding damn-be-to-you hand gestures, twisting and gyrating in a damning preacher-like body language. "It's a sin against *Gawwwd!*," he thundered. "Don't tell me this is a race issue. I grew up in the South and I know what racism is," blasting his words. "This isn't that and don't try to drag us blacks into it. The two are *NOT* connected."

He had a lot of moving parts going on. "One is a sin God abhors and the other is a wrong against a whole race," he said, sending shudders throughout the Assembly Hall. For his soul-shaking oration he received generous and overwhelming applause.

I listened to this gentleman with appreciation for his oratory skills, but boldly disagreed with every word he said. His oration pointed a moral finger at two of my fellow delegates, Sue and Mary, sitting a few rows in front of me. I thought of the conversation I'd had with them a few nights earlier.

After our Minnesota Caucus meeting on that first day a group of us went out to eat. We found a nice restaurant on Peachtree street, placed our order and chatted while we waited.

I struck up a conversation with Sue and the subject of marriage and divorce came up. I brought it up. I did my usual railing against the state of marriage. I noted my dad was married 36 years to my mom before she passed away from the ravages of diabetes. I was only 26 at the time. My aunt and uncle were happily married 60 years. I want that. As a single person in a messed up world, it's an uphill battle what with all the ugly marital war stories out there.

The topic of same-sex marriage found its way into the conversation. I railed about those pointing fingers. During a sermon at my church our pastor stated that while he knows same-sex marriage will be a legal reality soon in Minnesota, he doesn't want our church to judge, but to be inclusive, and invite those who choose that route to come and get introduced to Jesus. I personally believe in inclusion and non-judgment.

There seemed to be a connection between Sue and Mary, but I couldn't place it. Sue said that she'd been married once before. "It's not easy," she said, "and I've since remarried." References to Mary littered her sentences. Not putting two and two together, but suspecting something, I asked her to clarify her connection to Mary. "We're married," she said. After a pause she said, "We had to get married in Massachusetts because it wasn't yet legalized in Minnesota."

The internal fights in her family were sharp and heated. Her Grandpa refused to have anything to do with them. At family functions he wouldn't look at her if Mary was in the room. Arguments and tension became the norm.

Their church was no different. Their congregation had fierce objections and wanted the elders to do something; take action, kick them out. Kick some ass. Instead, the elders supported them, choosing to be inclusive to the Body of Christ.

In truth I seethed as I listened to that delegate. The beauty, the purpose of the Assembly is for debate to take hold, to listen to all points of view, however emotional, and to be allowed to have a say, too.

Were I to have turned in a slip and been chosen to speak I would have walked to the mic, grabbed it and said, "Sir, I respect you, what you are saying, and your beliefs in Christianity. But I couldn't disagree more with your words if I tried. I read the same Bible you do, and worship the same God you do. That same God who declares his hate for the sin of homosexuality also tells us not to judge others:

*And why worry about a speck in your friend's eye when you have a log in your own?*

That same God that you and I believe in loves us no matter our choices, like a parent loves a child. We should do the same!" I might not have the same thundering oratory skills that he did, but I can hold my own.

This was a powerful moment at the Assembly and worked its way into other conversations, including a lunchtime conversation across the street at the CNN Center Food Court. The lines were close to unbearable, especially the line for Salad Sensations, wrapping around kiosks and stretching into infinity.

I struck up a conversation with a small group of delegates also waiting in line at Salad Sensations, regaling them with my stories of the Mr Y BBQ Tour and my YouTube videos. This sparked their own take on barbeque and a little of their own history. One lady grew up in Tennessee, but teaches in Georgia—the other from Illinois.

Finding a seat in the Food Court presented a challenge. I found a way to sit with a couple of Illinois delegates, including the one I had talked to in line. The fiery preacher-like oration by that one delegate hadn't escaped their ears either.

They told the story of a gay teacher in Illinois who won the Gay Teacher of the Year Award for his excellent teaching. Both the principal and superintendent warned him he could mention his award as Teacher of the Year, but make no mention of the gay part. He ignored them and got fired. He left the teaching profession and is now involved in politics in some form.

"It's different in Minnesota," I told them. "In our own Minnesota delegation we have a same-sex married couple and we greet them with open arms. In my own school district one of our female education assistants is married to a female program supervisor. They are both well respected and great people. No big deal."

Both delegates shook their head in disbelief, their faces in mild shock. "Not in our state," they said in tones whispered so low that I strained to hear them.

The fact that the delegate with the fiery speech felt compelled to mention racism in his speech forced us here at the Assembly to confront a modern truth: Racism is alive and kicking.

The dream was that the Civil Rights Movement Dr. King spirited would have led to equality and that we wouldn't have the fitful overtones about race and race relations we still have today.

That first night, after eating, others offered to walk with me to the Black Caucus dance at the Marriott Hotel. It wasn't far from the restaurant. We waited for the stoplight to turn green at the intersection so that we could cross the street.

We observed two black men, one taller, one smaller screaming at a white suburbanite man. "You're noth'n but a white cracker!" They said it in a tone so dark and ugly it could darken the sun. The kept yelling this at him over and over, "You're noth'n but a white cracker!" The white guy kept going, ignoring the verbal mortar shells.

I didn't know the story behind their anger. The angry black men crossed to the other side of the road still in a rage. At various points they looked over at us sending fear our way. My concern heightened, as I was the same size and build as the white man they were screaming at. "Glad we're in a group," Mary whispered.

At the intersection Sue wanted to cross the street, placing us on the same side as the raging men. I silently forgave her for her lack of discernment and waited with patience for the light to change. It's sad this story is even there to tell.

# CHAPTER 9

The next day the line at Salad Sensations wrapped around kiosks again and stretched into infinity. My persistent sinus troubles were still bothering me and it drained the energy out of me. I got my salad and went to find a seat in the food court. I found no luck as the tables overflowed with lunchtime customers.

I searched and searched and almost gave up, but out of the corner of my eye I saw people starting to get up from a table in the center of the court. It was then that I first saw him, Big Mike. We had both spotted the same table, but from different directions, each eyeballing the open seats. We pounced at the same time, ending with him sitting across from me. I loved his story. It's better that mine.

Big Mike intrigued me. Not by his words, but by him, by the sheer force of his presence. A black man, he stood a large 6 ft 2 inches, perhaps a candidate for the health club. The bright red shirt and Falcons hat made him hard to miss.

I made a break from small talk by bragging that I'm an adjunct professor. I confided to Big Mike about the trials and tribulations of difficult students. I told him the story of one student who'd skipped out of class in the middle of it, and turned in all of her assignments on the last week rather than when they were due.

She suffered serious point deductions at my hands. During the last week she and I fought like cats and dogs. In the final class our dispute ended in a spectacle; she stormed out. I gave her an F for the course. She appealed it, and lost. Fail.

Somewhere in all that I slipped in that I also worked at a juvenile correctional facility with inner city youth. Big Mike grinned. He knew all too well my tale. Now it was his turn.

Big Mike had recently completed his Master's Degree in Social Work. His instructors didn't make it easy on him. In one class students complained to the administration that the instructor was too easy. The instructor didn't take kindly to this and assigned an in-class paper making them describe what they learned in her class. The instructor took those papers to the administration, telling them *this* is what her students learned. Student complaints about easy instructors were frequent in Big Mike's program.

When Big Mike told of another instructor his face got firm and his voice gained a steel thickness. That instructor had given him an A- instead of an A. "I missed by half a point," Big Mike gritted.

He fought back, telling the instructor, "I've never missed a class. I've never been late. I've turned in all my assignments. I've done well on all of them and gave you my best effort. Why are you doing this to me? I'm one of your best students. Others have missed classes and been real late, but you don't go after them." He lost that argument.

Big Mike faced me square. He planted his thick arms firm on the table and rolled his hands into fists. I witnessed solid anger when hearing his next tale. I sat quiet. I listened. He had taken an internship at a correctional facility and thrived there. They loved him, throwing him a party when he finished.

But his instructor got jealous, "They threw you a party, huh? I might not pass you Mike. That'll affect your disability status and that will affect your financial aid." You see, Big Mike had a disability and at one time lived on disability checks.

After collecting those checks for a while he decided,

"I ain't about that." Now, there was a jump in his voice. He leaned in close, where I could feel fierce intensity. It's here where the force of his personality took over. He scratched and clawed to get his degrees, he explained, driving over 100 miles one-way to get to class, never missing one, and showing the grit of a bulldog to finish.

What pissed him off so much is that his instructor had no appreciation whatsoever for what he went through to get to where he was. The jealousy of his instructor alone was enough to sink Big Mike.

"I got mad back. I fought back. I told him 'Why do you have to do that to me? You know I'm disabled.'" Big Mike's face wasn't far from mine. I was in the grips of his tale, on the edge of my seat, and rooting for him to win.

The instructor fired back his own volley, "You know Mike, you have to overcome obstacles. Things happen. You better advocate for yourself, Mike."

Big Mike, all revved up now, began to speak victory, "I've just started my first job, and it's at that correctional facility full-time. I love it. It's my passion. I'm looking into getting my PhD. I'm driven and I'm going to keep going." Somewhere, somehow, he'd picked himself up from the gutter and got going. He got mad. Got hungry. "I didn't always advocate for myself. I do now."

I made a connection with Big Mike. I could feel it. If you run into him and hear his story you'll get mad too. But in the end it will inspire you. You'll start advocating for yourself, and you'll be stronger for having met him. You'll say to your own obstacles, "I ain't about that."

Talking with Big Mike consumed hours rather than minutes. And I never did learn what his disability was. The Assembly had convened for lunch at noon, and would resume at 1 pm. Getting up from the table I checked the time—3 pm. I didn't have any great concerns as delegates routinely ignored the clock, coming and going at will.

I crossed the street to the plaza and proceeded

through the doors of the GWCC. I took my time, making a leisurely stroll down the long twisted hallways. The weight of my backpack again pulled on my shoulders. I had stuffed it to the hilt with pamphlets and paraphernalia. I cut through the Exhibition Hall like so many others as a shortcut to the Assembly Hall.

Halfway down I could see the outlines of the black curtains that hugged the entrance to the Assembly Hall. Friendly, smiling ushers manned the entrance. Then I heard it, faint at first, "*Roll Call* ... did somebody call for a Roll Call?" After a pause and some shuffling I heard, "... Okay, let's take a vote."

NOOOOO! I wanted to scream. I had taken too long for lunch. *Don't be stuck outside the Hall during a Roll Call*. Those words dinged through my head, leaving skid marks. This isn't going to look good. I'm a first time delegate. *I ain't about that.*

In an instant, a large group of delegates walking towards the Assembly Hall, like me, broke into a mad dash like a pack of zebras being chased by lions, thundering down the hallway in uncontrollable panic. The weight of my backpack slowed me down as my feet churned towards the entrance. We ran and chased as though in the midst of a race where the loser goes home.

"Okay, do we have a decision?" President Van Roekel blared. I accelerated into an all-out-turbo-charged sprint, looking more like Adrian Peterson blasting towards the goal line than an Education Assistant with bum knees.

"... All those who vote for Roll Call raise your hands." I could see the finish line, and the backs of other delegates. They ramped up their pace and so did I. I couldn't see a thing inside the Assembly. All I heard was, "All those against raise your hands." *Don't be stuck outside the Hall during a Roll Call*. I'm seconds away, don't do this to me, I thought.

The ushers moved closer to the curtains, readying themselves to stop us in the event the Roll Call passed. I stepped on the accelerator knowing I might have to dive to get in.

"Okay, we have a decision ..." I was ten steps away, the stinging words dug into me; not the thrill of victory, but the agony of defeat. "*Roll Call* ...." Please don't burn me. Four steps, three steps, two steps, "... *has been denied.*"

Whew! Our sprinting pack halted. Panic ceased. My shoulders throbbed from the backpack's bounce and pull. I began a slow, deliberate, almost cocky walk, passing the ushers on the way in. I smiled at them, knowing I'd have plowed them over if necessary to avoid my certain fate.

\* \* \*

After surviving those angry black men on the street on the way to the Marriott the night before, I found my way to the Black Caucus Dance. I purchased my ticket and strutted straight in.

The vibes were good, the music funky, and the food plentiful. It didn't matter that I was single and by myself; the party on the floor was open to all. I line-danced to country disco all night long. Once on the floor we were all family, no matter our abilities.

Being single and in search of meeting those of the other persuasion, I couldn't help but notice a woman grooving at a table near the food buffet. Dark hair, dark eyes, dark skin, she fit the profile. I guessed that she must have been Hispanic.

There is rarely a food buffet I don't agree with, and heading over there placed her in my sphere of influence. The buffet ran low so the attendant directed me to a second buffet on the other side of the ballroom. I noticed on my way over there that same Hispanic woman in front of me.

As she walked she grooved to the beat, swung her hips, and spun, like doing a pole dance. Her hair went flying. Ooohlala! Don't ask me how I know what a pole dance is like. I just know.

I made it to the second food buffet just behind her. Using a well tried conversation starter, I said, "Hi, I'm a first time delegate. Have you been a delegate before?"

She looked at me, paused, and said, "Yes," then walked away. That was it.

* * *

The first day of the Representative Assembly had seemed more like the Rolling Stones concert I attended back in 1995. 11,000 people all packed and revved. Music blared, balloons dropped, and confetti swirled as the masses clapped, cheered, whooped, whistled, and screamed as if it were their last breath.

Like many conventions there had been a parade of speeches, interrupted by applause, followed by more speeches, more applause, and more speeches. Something President Van Roekel said struck a chord—that in the course of making our kids better we don't want to look back and say, "We tried our best," or "we gave it our all." No, instead we want to say, "We did whatever it took."

Muhammad Ali used to say, "The will is stronger than the skill." When I think about it, the difference between a champion and runner up is usually very little. The champion digs in a little more, goes a little longer. He isn't satisfied with giving his "best effort." No, he or she "does whatever it takes."

The unfortunate thing about the Representative Assembly is that our state caucus meeting occurs first thing in the morning, seemingly at the crack of dawn. Early in the week the meetings started at 7 am. As the week progressed they started even earlier, at 6:30 am; an inconvenient truth.

At the restaurant that first night, Sue, a veteran delegate herself, alerted me to me how this whole NEA convention, Representative Assembly thing works. She said, "We may work by day, but it's party time at night. You'll see delegates during the Assembly who stayed up late just sit in their chair, eyes closed and head rolling from being so tired. They doze off because they can barely stay awake." She proceeded to mimic such a delegate, drooping and bobbing her head, rolling her eyes.

That very night I didn't go to bed at a reasonable hour. After the Black Caucus dance ended I made the long walk from the Marriott Hotel back to the Omni, hitting my pillow at something like 2 am. By the time I wound down from the buzz of the evening (I don't drink), it must have been close to 3 am. I remembered Sue's words, "... They doze off, they can barely stay awake." Nope, not going to happen to me, I thought. What a liar I was.

At the morning caucus meeting the next day I sat with droopy head, rolling my eyes, exactly as Sue had described other delegates. At the Assembly later on I wasn't much different. I pretended to comprehend the action before me and shook my head in simulated agreement, portraying the dual illusions of alertness and engagement. I even slithered down a slice of cantaloupe and gulped a blotch of orange juice in the desperate hope that they would help me generate a burst of energy.

In between my head drooping at the caucus and my fakery at the Assembly I strolled the corridors of the Exhibition Hall. It's there I had the most gripping and spirited discussion of the entire convention.

Nestled at the intersection of humanity and commerce sat the Christian booth. Each table in there contained stacks of books, DVDs, CDs, and the like. Ken Ham wrote or produced everything in there.

I admit I've never heard of him before, but I'm sure he creates a wide wake. Manning the booth were a Preacher and another gentleman.

The Preacher greeted me with a warm welcome. I began browsing the tables when he stepped over and said, "Take as many as you like, they're all free. The books are sold at $15 apiece if you bought them, but they're all free. They will show how science backs up the Bible, and answer common questions. We've brought along a PhD Astronomer to help explain the science." I shook the scientist's hand, my sole interaction with him.

This got me thinking. In the course of history there are those who have questioned the authenticity of the Bible and what it represents. Concerning other more secular books of history, such as on the Civil War or the Crusades, historians follow certain protocols and use specific metrics to authenticate what they are writing about.

I wondered how a modern historian in the 21st century could accurately quote Peter the Hermit, for example, during the first Crusade in the 11th century, some 1000 years earlier. They didn't have tape recorders or iPhones back then. The certain fact is that the modern historian quoting Peter the Hermit in a book published in 2010 wasn't there, and it would all have to be reliably passed on by word of mouth. How exactly does anyone know with accuracy what Peter the Hermit said?

One answer is that in each Crusade there were chroniclers who wrote down every aspect of the journey in exacting detail. They left nothing out, painting an amazing and accurate picture as events unfolded. What they wrote has been painstakingly preserved through the centuries, providing a proven, reliable history to modern historians.

I wondered why modern historians don't seem to apply the same protocols and metrics to the Bible as they do to a secular work of history.

Wouldn't this help to authenticate and answer some of the vexing questions we in the modern world have?

The Preacher stood and listened to me with arms crossed as I managed a long rambling tale:

"It's interesting your booth is here. I'd been thinking a lot about this kind of stuff lately. I remember having debates with fellow students when I was an engineering major at the University of Minnesota. It seems a scientist won't believe anything without hard scientific evidence. Isn't science man's explanation for what God has created?"

I could tell the Preacher liked this.

"I have friends who are agnostics," I continued, "We've had debates about the existence of God. They all say that someone needs to come to them with hard physical evidence and prove to them the existence of God. They reject the idea of believing on faith, i.e. believing without seeing.

I tell them, 'You can't see radio waves, but you believe they exist because you experience the effects of them, you hear something coming out of the radio.'"

I didn't intend to ramble as long as I was, but the Preacher didn't seem to mind. He kept standing there, arms crossed, listening intently to my tale. I suspected he'd heard this before.

"'No', my friends had responded. 'Using radio waves as an example doesn't prove anything. We need hard physical evidence,' they'd say.

'I don't get it,' I would tell them, 'isn't the existence or non-existence of God, a higher power if you will, isn't that pretty important?

Shouldn't you be proactively finding your own answers? You are sitting on a picket fence waiting for someone to come and prove it to you. But shouldn't you be the one finding your own answers? Isn't that important?'

'No,' they always responded, 'unless someone comes to me with hard physical evidence one way or the other, I can't make a decision. They have to come and bring it to me.'"

The Preacher shifted his weight from one leg to the other. He uncrossed his arms for the first time during my rambling. "I've had discussions with agnostics before, it's tough," he said, with a short frown. "Keep going, I want to hear more." He crossed his arms again, smiled, and kept listening.

"'Now wait a minute,' I had told one friend, who had been diagnosed with terminal colon cancer. 'You are a lot closer to finding out than the rest of us. Don't you think it's important to make a decision?'

'No. Someone needs to bring me hard evidence,' he said. 'I can't just believe on faith or on the word of what someone says.'

My friend was a math major and an expert, so I challenged him. 'Math isn't based on hard evidence, it's based on what some math guy said 300 years ago, but we're supposed to believe him. I can't see math, I can't touch it, but I'm supposed to believe it. How is that so?'

'Well,' he said, 'there are 7 math postulates that are the basis of all of math, created by math geniuses that everybody accepts are true geniuses.'

'Haha!' I said. 'You won't accept the Bible because you won't accept it on the faith of someone's word because you can't see it and touch it, but when it comes to math, we are supposed to believe it on the faith of some guy's word because he's really smart. That doesn't add up for me.'

'They're really smart.'

'That's weak,' I told him.

'Ok,' I said to those two agnostic friends who demanded hard physical evidence. 'I have a book I'll give you by Josh McDowell called *Evidence that Demands a Verdict*.

There's a follow-up book called *More Evidence that Demands a Verdict*. There's your hard physical evidence.' I gave them to the friend with terminal colon cancer first. He refused to look at them.

The other agnostic wouldn't look at them either. 'Wait a second. I don't get it,' I told the friend with cancer. 'You say you want evidence and I give you these books that show you hard physical evidence and you won't even open them.'

'Nope, don't have time.' The other friend said the same thing."

The Preacher, arms still crossed, absorbed the details of my tale with a vested interest. "Your story is fascinating. Like I said before I've had my own experiences with agnostics. Some of them just plain don't want to make a decision and they end up sitting on the picket fence forever. I've run into the same brick wall when I try to convince them to find answers. I applaud you for trying."

"Thanks for listening to me. Your booth got me thinking." I shifted gears. "You know, I'm a first time delegate at the convention next door. I haven't been to Atlanta since 1996. I came for the Olympics. It was phenomenal. I still remember the Southern hospitality. It's the same now. Amazing."

"Southern hospitality is part of the culture down here. It's amazing." I could tell by the look on his face he had something more on his mind. After a momentary pause he spoke. "It's funny," he said, "we come to this convention every year, wherever it is, and every year we get a stream of teachers that stop by and bad mouth us and curse and swear at us. They scream at us to leave and yell at us to not come back. Every year." He looked befuddled, unable to ascertain a reason for this.

I offered an explanation, "Sometimes, teachers are worse than kids. They can be the biggest brats. They're control freaks. Think about it. They control a classroom everyday loaded with misbehaving kids. They're used to being in control. Also, administrators sit on top of them ordering them around, so they're sandwiched between kids and administrators. On top of all that they're territorial. They don't take kindly to anyone messing with their classroom. Their rooms are their castle. Add it up. They can't blow off steam at school because they'd get in trouble. So they have to take it out on someone else and you're it."

The Preacher pondered my statements, "That makes sense. I hadn't thought of it that way, but it makes sense."

"How do you do it? Take that abuse. It must be brutal," I asked, wondering in genuine curiosity. I knew I couldn't do it.

He shrugged and gave me a sly, almost mischievous look. "We have thick skin. We're used to it. We can take it."

"Well," I said, "I've really enjoyed our chat, and I've picked out a bunch of different books from your booth and two DVDs. I'm going to be busy."

"You will," he said. "Help yourself to more if you want."

I thanked him one more time for the books and DVDs, and for listening to my tale, and bounded down the hallway.

# CHAPTER 10

Still in a need of a caffeine kick, I purchased a green tea at the kiosk along the hallway leading to the Assembly Hall. At first I thought it to be a Starbucks kiosk, but then realized I had passed a Starbucks store earlier in the hallway. Dressed in a light blue jean jacket, an attractive African-American barista worked the kiosk.

She was engaged in conversation with another customer. As I ordered my tea I couldn't help but notice the warm Southern charm she radiated. It's captivating. The $3.75 I paid for the tea sent small tremors down my spine until I realized I wasn't paying for it, my union was.

I couldn't help but overhear something in their conversation about food and barbeque. Interjecting myself, I said, "I love barbeque and everywhere I go I try some. Where is your favorite barbeque?" I struck gold. Her reply came back Smithfield's Bar-B-Q in Fayetteville and the Cook-Out in Greensboro, both in North Carolina.

The other customer, greedy for her attention, shooed me away in a most gentlemanly manner. Not given a choice I grabbed my tea and started to leave. Her warm Georgia Peach personality continued to fill the hallway behind me. Holding the cup up to my mouth I took a sip, burning my tongue. I should film her, I thought.

I sloshed down more of those $3.75 teas in my war to stay awake. It's amazing my lack of concern for cost when it's someone else's dime. When the Assembly ended for the day I could barely move down the hallways. I took shuffled steps, each heavier than the one before. My head and shoulders slumped. I could feel the weight of my eyelids drooping, the fatigue in unrelenting overdrive.

As I pushed through the exit doors I headed straight across the street to CNN Center where my tour started in minutes. I couldn't figure out a better time to take the tour than now because I had a rigid schedule and I was sticking to it, despite my semiconscious state.

I rail all the time about the state of news in our modern world. It's usually an endless stream of negatives. It's become too sensationalized and tabloid. News organizations exert great influence, and it's as though they are in a contest to see who can screw up our minds the most.

I am not the first to feel this way. On April 14, 1906, President Theodore Roosevelt attacked the media over their penchant for tabloid sensationalism in his famous, *The Man with the Muck Rake* speech, delivered at the laying for the cornerstone for the Cannon Office Building in Washington D.C. He did a more-than-commendable job. It's from this speech "Muckraker" became a coined term:

> *In Bunyan's "Pilgrim's Progress" you may recall the description of the Man with the Muck Rake, the man who could look no way but downward, with the muck rake in his hand; who was offered a celestial crown for his muck rake, but who would neither look up nor regard the crown he was offered, but continued to rake to himself the filth of the floor.*

> *he also typifies the man who in this life consistently refuses to see aught that is lofty, and fixes his eyes with solemn intentness only on that which is vile and debasing. Now, it is very necessary that we should not flinch from seeing what is vile and debasing.*

> *There is filth on the floor, and it must be scraped*

*up with the muck-rake; and there are times and places where this service is the most needed of all the services that can be performed. But the man who never does anything else, who never thinks or speaks or writes, save of his feats with the muck-rake, speedily becomes, not a help to society, not an incitement to good, but one of the most potent forces for evil.*

*The men with the muck-rakes are often indispensable to the well-being of society; but only if they know when to stop raking the muck, and to look upward to the celestial crown above them, to the crown of worthy endeavor. There are beautiful things above and round about them; and if they gradually grow to feel that the whole world is nothing but muck, their power of usefulness is gone.*

*Hysterical sensationalism is the poorest weapon wherewith to fight for lasting righteousness. The men who with stern sobriety and truth assail the many evils of our time, whether in the public press, or in magazines, or in books, are the leaders and allies of all engaged in the work for social and political betterment. But if they give good reason for distrust of what they say, if they chill the ardor of those who demand truth as a primary virtue, they thereby betray the good cause.*

It's impossible to avoid knowing you're at CNN Center. A humongous, gigantic, huge-ola size TV screen adorns the center courtyard broadcasting CNN News 24/7. This is not an understatement. It looms and dominates.

The courtyard escalator is the world's largest stand-alone escalator. At one time CNN Center was some sort of hotel development replete with water slides until Ted Turner purchased the whole thing and turned it into CNN. Looking up, I could see the old hotel rooms, still fitted with balconies, that are now offices.

We toured a simulated news studio where a little tyke on our tour read fake news into a camera using a teleprompter. He did pretty well. We toured their news studios, craning our necks to see someone famous. We checked out the anchor desks, and headed down to the newsrooms where writers and editors worked in diligent fashion to bring us the stories that get us depressed. For major news stories up to 300 employees cram the desks.

The newsroom looks just like it does in the movies. Desks, monitors, and computers are jammed everywhere. Writers stuff chairs gliding their fingers across keyboards in efficient action. Bodies roam the hallways grasping sheets of paper in one hand and a pen in the other.

A pencil is always shoved behind their ear. Their head is always down, scribbling notes as they move. Text, pictures and video slide across the monitors in constant motion. CNN owns an amazing ability to monitor the world and tell us about it in an instant, all proofread and streamlined to fit between the commercials in our uber-busy mile-a-minute lives.

When the tour finished we ended up, predictably, in the souvenir shop. A familiar feeling arose. Determined this time to get it right and purchase one low-cost t-shirt I stuck to my guns, until I saw the mugs. Staggering from the cashier and ready for a nap, I grabbed the bag filled with my purchases and hobbled off to the hotel.

I awoke from my nap moderately refreshed. I headed downtown for dinner and passed a life-size bronze statue of Mayor Andrew Young adorning International Boulevard. More memories of 1996. I searched for restaurants and settled on an Indian place not far from the statue.

I ordered a plate of Basmati rice and chicken, with a side order of Naan bread. Naan bread is the best. I consumed it heavily when I went to India. The total bill came to a staggering $30. I wasn't paying for it, so it shouldn't matter, but sorry to say, a tinge of Catholic guilt worked its way in. It shouldn't have cost more than $15, with tip, considering it was basically a side order of rice and bread. Even on someone else's dime that darn guilt makes a run at it, working to outweigh the fun.

I staggered back to my hotel room near exhaustion with not an ounce of energy. I remembered I had brought *Red Shift, Blue Shift* along. I grabbed it and headed downstairs to read, plopping in a chair at the bar with the singular intent of ordering a Diet Coke.

"Hey, weren't you at the toga party?" a mysterious voice said. I looked up to see two women grinning at me. "I was at the toga party and I saw you wearing a toga," one of them, Margaret, said. She had short brown hair and wore a black dress. In her mid to late thirties, she was a first-time delegate from another midwestern state.

"Yes, that was me," I replied. Our Minnesota caucus held a toga party the night before where we were to wear our bed sheet as a toga. I sort of cheated in that I simply wore the bed sheet over the top of my shirt.

The other, Barbara, had medium length tanish brown hair, and was outfitted with a light colored dress. In her early to mid thirties, she also was a first-time delegate, hailing from a mid-south state.

Soon, the topic turned to how we became delegates. I said, "The sum total of how I became a delegate is that I went to our school coffee shop one day to order a cooler. and the co-worker working the counter, our union rep, said to me, 'Hey, your name came up at the union meeting. Do you want to be a delegate to the NEA convention to Atlanta in July?'"

"Who's paying for it?"

"The union."

"I'm in!"

"Are you kidding me?" Margaret exclaimed, "I had to campaign against others and I had to find a grant because our union didn't have any money." She looked like she wanted to punch me.

"I had to go up against others, too," Barbara said. "I did a lot of work to become a delegate. How is your union organized?"

"Well, we don't have really any structure. I'm a delegate for my local union, and then there are state delegates," I answered.

"In our state we're organized into zones, and then regions, and then districts." Barbara's face displayed a perceptible amount of stress.

"In Minnesota each district has basically their own union," I said. "The union I'm a delegate for is the union for my school district. There aren't any zones or anything."

"In our state we have regions, zones, and districts," Barbara continued, using hand motions to give a visual. Each time she spoke she locked eyes with firm intensity onto the eyes of the person she was speaking to. "Regions, zones, and districts," she repeated. "I had to get elected in the regions first, giving speeches and everything, then zones, and districts. I had to go to events and do a lot of work to get elected." Her stress level had risen to a level beyond perceptible, bordering on anxiety.

I noticed that her previously full glass of alcoholic beverage was on its way to becoming empty. She didn't stop there, "I've been a teacher for nine years. My school is small, and I do everything. I teach all the way from fifth grade to high school. My kids come from poor rural families. They don't have any money and I have to buy stuff all the time. I do all the work. I work my butt off." The rhythm of her pace picked up considerable speed, like when the fast-forward button is hit on a tape deck. With her glass of alcoholic beverage now empty she ordered another one.

Margaret is a linguist pathologist. A fancy term that means she helps kids with speech, vocabulary, and pronunciation issues. She opined that her school principal didn't do a thing except run around and schmooze all day.

Barbara joined in, "My principal doesn't do a thing all day either. He just sits in his office all day. I can do better than him." The sips from her glass increased in frequency, to a more than steady pace. Her facial expressions increased, too, "I have a Masters Degree in Science. I do everything at my school. I don't have any free time. I go, go, go all day long. I went back to school to get a degree to be a principal." She paused for a second or two to steal a couple of sips from her glass. She continued, prosecuting her case like an attorney, "I am. I am going to be a principal. I'm going to be a good one. I am." Adding fuel to her fire, and a few more sips to her belly, She continued, "I'm applying for principal jobs, but didn't find one for this year. I'm going to keep applying. I'm going to find one. I am. I'm going to teach for another year and keep applying. I'm going to find one. I am," forcing us to accept her ambitions. She added one more stick to the fire, "I'm the union president, too!"

She didn't need us to validate her next career choice or convince us she was ambitious. It was self-evident. Her passion, her heart for her kids spoke louder than any words could. Her drive to be the best was fortunate for any kid entering her classroom, and the world of education should be on its knees in gratitude.

It didn't take much to notice that the more she spoke, the more she prosecuted her case. The more she prosecuted her case, the more her ambitions rose to the surface. The more her ambitions rose to the surface, the more her anxieties had a field day. The more her anxieties had a field day, the more she spoke at a fast-forward clip. The more she spoke at a fast-forward clip, the more sips she took. And the more sips she took, the more she was on a path to silly.

The topic of administrators is always a sensitive one. In many cases the administrator running the school used to be a teacher there. There are concerns that the power might go to their head. Margaret recounted for us her experience of a fellow teacher who changed upon becoming an administrator.

To illustrate her indignation she asked a rhetorical question to thin air, as though the former teacher, now administrator, was standing right there, "Remember two years ago, when you were one of us?" She made no attempt to hide her mocking tone. She equated the new found power of that former teacher with course sandpaper.

A man, Bob, appeared out of nowhere and introduced himself. A fellow co-worker of Barbara's, he added a lightness to the nighttime air. Bob and Margaret seemed to hit if off immediately, heading into the topic of love. This arena hasn't been a strength of mine, so I sat and listened with passionate interest, hoping to pick up a few pointers.

Margaret began the conversation, "I've dated Mark for two years and recently split up with him. He'd told me for the last six months that I'd been treating him like crap, and I admit that I have. After I broke it off with him he came over for the *big talk*. I told him that we're done, that 'I'm going through some things right now and I don't know where I'll come out.' But he doesn't get it! He thinks this is a temporary break."

Bob pressed her for her reasons to not to want to be with Mark. She continued, "He has a 13 year-old-kid. I'm a special ed teacher, and I don't approve of the way he is raising his son. I have my act together. I have a job. I own my own house. He doesn't have his act together. He's put me on this pedestal and doesn't get it that we're through."

Barbara listened in, but soon went back to relieving herself of her anxieties.

Bob asked Margaret, "He doesn't get that you two are through?"

"No he doesn't," she said, "I don't get why. I was clear."

"I don't think you were clear," Bob said. "You're sending conflicting messages."

"You have to just cut it, no wiggle room," I chimed in, breaking my vow of silence.

"But I was clear," Margaret defended, "I couldn't have been more clear when I said, '*We're through.*'"

"Yes, but you left wiggle room when you said you didn't know where you'd come out," Bob said.

"When I listen to you I'm confused, too" I added, "and I'm not even involved. What do you think Mark is thinking?"

Margaret defended herself again, "I *was* clear. I did cut it off. He has me on a pedestal, he won't move on. I have my act together. I have a job and own my own home. He doesn't have his act together. He works on commission. One day he might be making good money and the next minimum wage." Bob and I listened to her like tag team counselors. "I'm thirty-seven years old, I have my act together. I want to have kids. Mark might be my last chance."

I knew the truth. I've been in Mark's shoes; a hold-me-over until something better comes along, a security blanket against loneliness with no real interest down the line. When something better comes along, Mark is out the door. The poor fellow. He won't know what hit him.

"I'm not even involved and I'm confused," Bob counseled, "Mark doesn't have any idea what's going on. He probably thinks you'll come back. You have to cut the cords completely and let him move on. He isn't your last chance. I'm 43 and I've been married twice before and was recently engaged until she broke it off out of the blue."

Margaret defended, "I'm thirty-seven. I'm getting up there. I don't know how many more chances I'll get. I feel like Mark might be my last chance. I want to have kids. He might be my last chance ... how old are you?" She looked straight at me.

"Fifty-three."

"See. This might be might be my last chance."

Spurious thoughts racked my brain. Every day presents amazing opportunity. Lose sight of that and doom descends. Life depends on the six-inches between our ears. Gandhi said it best: *The future only depends on what I do right now.*

"No, it's not your last chance," I insisted, not convinced my words had any effect. I reflected internally on a passage in the Bible, Matthew Chapter 7, verses 7-10:

*Keep on asking, and you will receive what you ask for. Keep on seeking, and you will find. Keep on knocking, and the door will be opened to you.*

I gave it one more go. "When I listen to you I'm confused," I pressed. "And if I'm confused, what do you think Mark is feeling? It's not fair to him. You have to make a clean cut and get rid of the wiggle room."

It appeared I made no dent in her stance. Seeing it was 1:30 am, and Bob and Margaret were warming up to each other, I turned my attention to Barbara. I wasn't ready to head back to my room so I slithered down some sips of Diet Coke and readied myself to engage her in conversation for continued fun.

Sillier by the second and encapsulated in her own little world, she slithered more tonic down her throat, convinced this would cure her anxieties. She giggled and slurred, leaning in close, saying, "We might have to sneak back to our rooms," clutching her glass and breaking a smile.

It was now up to me to save the day and rescue Mark. I implored Barbara, "Can you talk some sense into Margaret? She thinks Mark is her last chance. He isn't, and she wants to have kids with him. Bob and I aren't getting through to her. She's not listening. She'd be making a big mistake."

Barbara, despite her silliness, offered practical action, "She's got to come to her senses. It would be the biggest mistake ever to have a kid with Mark if she doesn't want to be with him. Big mistake. I'll have a girl talk with her and talk some sense into her."

"Thanks," I said, as I paid the bartender for my Diet Coke. I slinked away hoping I had made the world a better place. A strange course of thinking happened to me on the way back to my room. In spite of being involved in an intense relational crisis, I couldn't shake thoughts of Thelma's Kitchen.

Something about that hole-in-the-wall infected me to the point that I couldn't for the life of me get it out of my brain. After I had seen the shadows of them by the freeway the other night I had done some internet research. It said they were the best soul food in Atlanta. Down home. Earthy. Original. An Atlanta institution. Their Yelp reviews were off the charts.

# CHAPTER 11

The closest I got to the mic during the entire week was that I volunteered to be a yielder. I became a ping pong ball in the political gamesmanship to get New Business Item 77 passed. Our Minnesota caucus supported it and teamed up with other caucuses.

Prior New Business Items got tabled to a committee, so they never came up for a vote. Due to this it came down to an interpretation of what "five Items before" meant. To our caucus president, since some Items were tabled, "five Items before" meant Item 65. To the attendant calling in the slips at the microphone "five items before" meant 77 minus 5 equals Item 72.

I hustled up to the attendant, "Here's my slip for Item 77. My caucus president said we could turn it in on Item 65."

The attendant said, "I'm sorry, I can't. You have to wait until Item 72."

I hustled back to our caucus president, who sent me back with marching orders. I said to the attendant, "I spoke with my caucus president, and she said ...."

The attendant held her ground, "I'm sorry. I can't call this in."

Shuttling back again to my caucus president, her temperature rose a bit. "*You tell her* ...," and off I went to the microphone.

The attendant didn't budge an inch from our demands, "... that's what the moderator may have said before the break, but we were told after the break that ...."

Back and forth, back and forth I went in a merry-go-round of edicts and refusals. On my last trek up there, I said, "You know, I'm like a ping-pong ball here. The left isn't talking to the right. My president says one thing, and you say another." I smiled at her. "At this point it's irrelevant; we're only a couple of numbers away. I'm just going to stay here until we're called."

"Yeah, we're almost there," she said.

I'm not the most astute political operative in the world. Another nearby delegate spoke on item 77, in opposition to our caucus's view. "Hey, good job," I said to her, "I teach communications and I'm always preaching short and sweet and you were very short. Very effective! I know we're on opposite sides of the coin here, but that doesn't matter. Good presentation."

"Thanks," she said, smiling.

President Van Roekel cut off debate. My moment of glory faded. All I can claim is that I partook in the game and am the better for it. The Assembly voted down New Business Item 77.

"See, short and sweet is better isn't it? You guys got us on this one, way to go," I said to the delegate opposed as I headed back down the aisle.

The great fun is that Captain America made an appearance at our caucus, at the hotel, and at the Assembly. Fundraising is a big deal and Captain America made every effort to empty our pockets for the cause. I paid money to wear a red, white, and blue cowboy hat and an American Flag cape.

Ms. Rinker, my fellow union delegate, couldn't resist and snapped a picture, posting it on Facebook. Later in the afternoon she asked me, "Do you have a friend Rich or something like that?"

"Yes," I said, befuddled. *How does she know Rich?* I've known him since high school. He lives in Columbus, Ohio. I've never uttered his name at work before.

Chuckling, Ms. Rinker said, "He responded when I posted your picture. You should read it, something about being socialist."

"Oh, Rich!" I said, remembering his political persuasions. "He's a conservative. He listens to Rush Limbaugh."

"You have to read his post, it's so funny!"

Of course, the first thing I did when I got back to the hotel after the Assembly was to fire up Facebook and find the post:

*Tim, I didn't know that you are a member of a left wing, socialist organization like the NEA.*

I replied:

*Who doesn't like a good left wing? In fact, Fox Bros. BBQ has the best left wing in Atlanta.*

Only Rich, I thought, only Rich. I've known him since the ninth grade when we both went to Oak Grove Junior High in Bloomington, Minnesota, and then Kennedy Senior High. After high school he went to North Dakota State University in Fargo, while I attended the University of Minnesota in the Twin Cities.

I have fond memories of our all-night Risk games in high school, especially on New Year's Eve where we linked *two* boards together. I still use the Australia strategy to this day. During college I made an occasional trek up to Fargo in the blistering cold to visit him. The temperature in those parts during winter averaged −4 F with a wind chill of −16 F. *Brrrrrr.*

We've stayed in touch over the years and it's been a blessing to have him as a friend. He spent many years in the Army and Army Reserve as a helicopter pilot and did a tour of duty in Iraq and one at the Mexican Border. Currently, in real time, he is flying relief duty in Puerto Rico after Hurricane Maria.

His conservative views are in contrast to my more liberal views, but it's always enlightening to compare and contrast our different viewpoints.

Rich has a point though. One of the stated goals of the Assembly is that we, the NEA, fight for social justice. It's more than just what happens in the classroom. We throw our weight around. We're more liberal than conservative; more Ron Paul than Rush Limbaugh.

The beauty of the NEA is that it is a true blue democratic process. All voices are heard. All points of view are considered. Delegates decide every little thing. Nothing moves forward unless we say so.

This is the first time I'd been an active participant in any sort of political convention. I found myself supporting some issues and others not so much. Sometimes I voted liberal and sometimes I voted conservative. Our caucus leaders said to vote the way we wanted regardless of our official Minnesota caucus position. I took their advice to heart. In the political world I'm a centrist. I don't need to defend myself do I?

Coming back from lunch one day I again saw that woman from the Black Caucus party. She was walking to the Assembly Hall with a group of her fellow delegates. She stopped and took a picture of a poster near an escalator while the others went ahead.

I seized the opportunity for a second chance. I approached her, using another tried and true conversation starter, "What state are you a delegate of?" I assumed she was a California delegate, for I'd seen her strolling about the California section a lot.

She gave me a puzzled dirty look when she said, "I'm from the Pacific Islander caucus."

"Oh," I said, "I didn't know there was a Pacific Islander caucus. Pacific Islander as in Pacific Ocean?"

"Pacific Islander caucus," she said terse. Her body language said it all: *go away.*

"I'm sorry, I didn't know." I'm swimming upstream against the current, I thought.

After the Assembly ended for the day I headed back

to my hotel room at a good clip. I didn't have time for anything more than to grab a sweatshirt. Our bus heading for the Atlanta Braves baseball game at Turner Field would be leaving in a few minutes. Our Minnesota delegation was headed there as a Special Night Out event.

I knew a flood of nostalgia would return well before we arrived at the stadium. 1996 was a special year. But it's never the same seeing something a second time after creating a lifetime of memories the first time.

Turner Field had aged by seventeen years although the colonial brown brick and the bustling concourses didn't seem to. The smell of beer and brats never gets old. It's baseball, American style. What made it different now is that it was nighttime, rainy and overcast. Each of us delegates bought an all-you-can-eat club seat costing a stiff $60. That's one thing that was different. The prices were much higher. And Captain America was slated to make an appearance. The food wasn't particularly high quality, but it did have bulk.

The game itself, played between drops of rain, didn't create any new or lasting memories. The delegate sitting behind me did. With every thrust of the ball and every swing of the bat he'd yell at the top of his lungs. He spared no one. I thought I could handle the decibels, but over time I realized I, too, am mortal.

Infused with Minnesota Nice, I faked like I had to get up and get more food from the buffet. Coming back I used the opportunity to sit in the next section, away from the very loud delegate.

It mattered not that I sat in the drizzly rain, at least I wasn't near him. But not for long. An usher shooed me back because, "You can't eat food in this section, you have to stay in your section."

I looked around and observed a very empty stadium. I considered putting up a fuss, but didn't. This put me back within shouting distance. He continued yelling without mercy for anyone.

I soon saw other delegates get up and move two sections over underneath the upper deck overhang to get cover from the rain (or *him*). I followed suit, but not before I seized the day and filmed the delegate with the mouth. He did a superb job, ratcheting it up a decibel or two for my small YouTube audience.

Later, he followed us over to the covered section. Perhaps concerned for our eardrums he ceased his yelling, and watched the game along with the rest of us as just an ordinary citizen.

Sitting in my seat and dozing in and out consciousness from the sufferings of little sleep, I found myself reflecting on that morning's caucus meeting. It proved to be the most emotionally charged of the entire week, all due to New Business Item 93. It urged the NEA to oppose the name "Redskins" as the team name for the Washington Redskins NFL team.

It had been the last New Business Item at the Assembly the day before. I had missed the floor debate, but Ms. Rinker said it was "the most hotly debated Item of the day." Emotional, explosive, and divisive.

As Ms. Rinker explained, the term "Redskins" was referred to as institutional racism. Andrew Jackson, our seventh president (yes, he's the one who shipped Native Americans wholesale to the western frontier), coined the term in reference to Indian scalps. In some circles this term is equated to the N-word.

It's from this vantage point that our morning caucus debate took place. One delegate gave an impassioned, tear-filled plea. Another delegate, a man of Native American heritage, gave us insight into how the Native American community viewed this term.

He acknowledged that the issue divides the Native American community, but gave us his own personal views. It propagates stereotypes of earlier centuries, he said, specifically the era of Cowboys and Indians, and denigrates Native Americans. "Look at the symbolism used when you go to the Braves game tonight. Look at how they portray Native Americans. Be aware and observe the team mascot, the tomahawk chop, the music, the dress ... everything," he urged.

In 1991 the Minnesota Twins played the Atlanta Braves in the World Series. "Stop the Chop," became a familiar rallying cry. Native Americans protested on the plaza in front of the Hubert H. Humphrey Metrodome. On one occasion I joined them.

While this is a hot button issue, it doesn't preclude me from attending a sporting event, despite what a team's name might or might not be. So far, I've found myself indifferent. Nobody seems to object to the Notre Dame Fighting Irish, but the debate is splitting when it comes to the North Dakota Fighting Sioux.

There's a famous song entitled *Dirty White Boy* and a band of the same name. I could careless that white caucasian males, of which I'm one, are referred to this way. But I get and appreciate the struggles of the Native American community and the offense they take. Over the centuries they've been cheated, hustled, swindled, denigrated, beaten, and hunted down by the white man.

It's this frame of mind I had as I sat in my seat in Turner Field in the cold drizzling rain. I made note of all the things the Native American delegate advised us to note; the mascot, the tomahawk chop, the music, the dress ... everything. What I observed didn't roll down a boulder of indignation for me, but I did gain awareness.

Recently, Dan Snyder, owner of the Washington Redskin's, published an editorial outlining his reasons for sticking with the name "Redskins."

In it he said the term connotes bravery and strength and he gave specific examples. However, the majority of the Native American community responded to his editorial in a negative way.

Recently some newspaper publishers and journalists issued press releases stating they will no longer use the term "Redskins" in any way, shape, or form out of solidarity with the Native American community. The moral of the story is that the debate goes on and it isn't slowing down anytime soon. All I can claim is that I'm more aware, and carefully listening. And for me, that's a good start.

I felt good after scoring an Atlanta Braves hat for $5 from a tent bordering the parking lot where our bus waited. The rainy overcast night continued to drop a dreary drizzle in the air. The heat in Atlanta, while on hold for days, had been on the rise lately making for stifling hot, humid conditions.

On the way back to the hotel our bus stopped at a red light. Looking left through the bus window I noticed a parking ramp. I observed that in every stall homeless people had setup for the night. With nowhere else to go the ramp provided shelter for them. Most had either a sleeping bag or blanket. Some had neither. A torrent of emotions came pouring from me, and a sickening emptiness filled my stomach; gut wrenching at best.

Earlier in the week I had seen the other end of the spectrum: fancy custom homes decorating plush green lawns with sprawling gardens and flower beds, with shiny new Beamers and Mercedes-Benzes lining the driveways.

But here, from the window of my bus, I witnessed the desperation to stay alive. To exist. I felt a certain guilt. It held no relation to Catholic guilt. It ran deeper. I questioned the humanity of what I saw. A speaker at the Assembly raised this issue.

He challenged those who would say this was mere collateral damage in our capitalist system. A poor excuse and wrong, he said.

I had seen this misery before in cities like Washington D.C. and St. Louis. Ditto for Central Asia, India, and Indonesia. It doesn't get any easier nor do the emotions die. It's the same every time, the unfairness, the disbelief that some have so much while others struggle for survival. It transcends all economic systems; no one system adequately solves the problem.

Moral questions rise up. Is society to blame? What's their story? Drugs? Alcohol? Broken families? How much is on their shoulders? How much is on my shoulders?

But I won't be mad at the well-to-do in Alpharetta—they aren't evil. They didn't cause those people to be in the parking stalls. The well-to-do work hard, take risks, take care of their families, create commerce, and generate opportunities. I applaud them for their success. It's part of our human condition to want to get ahead. Nobody wants to be poor. It's why we go to school or start a business or invent something or make investments. It'd be wrong if we didn't.

I'm not a believer in the idea that the less I have the more saintly I am. Nor do I believe that in order to be happy I have to be poor. Nor is making money a moral issue for me. I feel much better when I have a generous bank account. I like not having to sweat bullets when I need money for a brake job. I jump for joy when I can pay for a trip in cash.

Success is golden. It's wonderfully energizing. But in a bold way, giving a little bit of myself or spending a small sum for the benefit of someone else is the happiest money I spend.

Those people in the parking ramp deserve a chance. A chance to change, a chance to get clean, a chance to live and thrive and have their dreams come true, like the rest of us. And now for my soapbox. You knew it was coming. Pity isn't what's needed. Love and compassion are.

A lot of people each giving a little bit can make a big difference. Think about when a national tragedy happens and lots of us rally and make small donations to a Go-FundMe account or something similar. It's a good feeling when we learn hundreds-of-thousands of dollars have been raised to make a difference, yet we each only gave a little. That's all I'm suggesting. Together, when we add it all up, we create a difference maker, an agent of change. We'll feel good that we made a difference, without having to rob ourselves to do it.

I finally got back to my room at the hotel still percolating with emotions. I felt a pang of thirst and grabbed the bottle of Acqua Panna natural spring water sitting on the desk. I gripped the bottle tight in one hand and reached with the other to twist open the cap. Just before I started to twist I hesitated, noticing a small asterisk, with *$6.00* printed next to it. I pulled the bottle close and read the small print ... *A charge will be billed to your room if consumed.*

I rubbed my eyes to make sure I had read it correctly. I did. Those sneaks. It's not enough the room costs $165 per night. They know I'm going to be tired late at night, thirsty, and instinctively grab the bottle and slug it down. Bam! Ka-ching! Done.

I put the bottle back on the desk and let go. I saw their ruse and beat them, this time. It's bad enough everyone tries to nickel and dime me. Now they've gone upscale, trying to dollar and five-dollar me too.

I hopped in my plush bed and pulled the covers over, thankful I'm living the high life, if only for a moment. Blocks away, my fellow man struggled for survival, grateful he's got a cold slab of concrete to sleep on in the scorching humidity. The cool dry air in my room stayed that way through the night, regulated by the computerized thermostat on the wall. The unfairness, the gut wrenching moral wrong, paused my ability to sleep. But not for long.

I got up in the morning and headed over to the Assembly after our caucus meeting. I noticed someone had moved the kiosk with the high priced teas to the top of the escalator leading to the Assembly Hall. Buying teas from this kiosk and drinking them had become my method of choice to stay awake.

The barista working the kiosk was the same one from before, the one who gave me her favorite barbeque places. She chatted as pleasantly as always, decked to the nines in a blue patterned dress and jean jacket. Somewhere in the random conversations I heard her mention an audition later that night to another customer.

When the Assembly ended for the day I walked by the kiosk and, remembering about her audition, threw her some encouragement. "I hope you do really well at your audition tonight. I hope you nail it."

"Thanks. I'm auditioning for a lead role." she said, warm and appreciative.

"You're going to come in here tomorrow and tell me you nailed it!"

She broke into a big smile, and like a student making a promise to her teacher said, "Okay, I will."

# CHAPTER 12

Lack of sleep is the new normal when attending a convention like this. Dozing off is how we cope. The alarm goes off between 5:30 am and 6:00 am. A continental breakfast is served during the morning caucus, which starts at 6:30 am sharp. After that we head over to the Assembly.

If we're lucky enough to get through all the business items, the proceedings end around 5 pm. If not, we stay late. Then it's dinner and off to a night of fun and frolic, coming home in the wee hours, only to start the cycle all over again the next day.

We do serious business during the Assembly. We make decisions that affect every child in America. We decide things like STEM or STEAM. Art electives are being cut everywhere and in order to find a niche for themselves art teachers are looking to provide added value by infusing their own brand of creativity into tech curriculums, thus the A in STEAM.

Some states have watered down the 1965 Civil Rights Act, stripping out certain voting rights for minorities. We had to decide how to put our foot down on this. Immigration reform, sexual orientation, classroom diversity, high stakes testing, these are just some examples of the kind of serious business that we vote on. We expend significant emotional currency in doing so.

Some New Business Items are meant to be serious, but are a fail. Take New Business Item 20 for example:

*The term "Educator" in the award name is chosen to reflect that across the nation, higher edu-*

*cation professional faculty go by many names:*

*professor, lecturer, instructor, counselor, librarian, and a host of other names. It does NOT, nor is intended to include those former faculty who have gone over to the dark side as administrators, deans, or other defectors to the profession.*

Am I wrong?

In another New Business Item it was requested of the NEA that when they book conventions they only choose hotels that have secure smoking areas for delegates so they won't be bothered by homeless people or be asked for money by vagrants. This resulted in a firestorm and ended in boos. Our caucus leaders told us to never boo out of respect. I confess I joined the chorus of boos, and it felt damn good.

Towards the end of the convention we had perplexing matters to attend to. Three constitutional amendments were on the table:

- *Constitutional Amendment 1: To change the percentage of classroom teachers required on NEA committees from seventy-five (75) percent to the percentage of classroom teachers within the NEA membership, with certain exceptions.*
- *Constitutional Amendment 2: To remove the teacher percentage requirement for NEA committees.*
- *Constitutional Amendment 3: To change the percentage of classroom teachers required on NEA committees from at least seventy-five (75) percent to at least sixty (60) percent.*

Each amendment was a variation of the same thing. This was unprecedented, President Van Roekel explained. He invoked Robert's Rules of Order to solve the dilemma. He offered two solutions:

- Option 1: We debate amendments 1, 2, 3 and then hold a secret vote; majority wins.
- Option 2: We have a playoff system and whittle the amendments down to one, then hold a secret vote on this one amendment.

He opened the floor for debate. After he closed the debate we had a floor vote to decide on which option to go with. Option 2 won. After the vote ended *someone* called Division, and then *someone else* called for a Roll Call.

I couldn't believe it! After all the discussions and all the debates and all the votes, a select few had the audacity to storm the microphones, challenging the whole process as unconstitutional, an abuse of power, a slippery slope.

I sat flabbergasted. An entirely democratic process had been used. There had been an open floor debate followed by a floor vote. It can't get any more democratic than that! The main problem was that these challenges occurred at the end of a very long day. No one wanted to listen to them. Another chorus of boos ensued, and I joined right in.

President Van Roekel did a masterful job of shutting down these challengers, invoking his rights as president under Robert's Rules of Order. Per Option 2, we held a playoff and got it down to Constitutional Amendment 2, to be decided the next morning by secret vote. And that was that.

I found the idea that we adhered to Robert's Rules of Order intriguing, and did a little research:

from (robertsrules.com)

the Official Robert's Rules of Order website

*Henry Martyn Robert was an engineering officer in the regular Army. Without warning he was asked to preside over a public meeting being held in a church in his community and realized that he did not know how. He tried anyway and his embarrassment was supreme. This event, which may seem familiar to many readers, left him determined never to attend another meeting until he knew something of parliamentary law.*

*Ultimately, he discovered and studied the few books then available on the subject. From time to time, due to his military duties, he was transferred to various parts of the United States, where he found virtual parliamentary anarchy, since each member from a different part of the country had differing ideas of correct procedure. To bring order out of chaos, he decided to write Robert's Rules of Order, as it came to be called.*

A curious thing happened earlier in the morning, between the end of the caucus and the start of the Assembly. I had headed over to CNN Center to get cash from an ATM machine. I had carried a poster with me. Barely awake, I'd gone to the nearest cash machine, inserted my card, punched some buttons, and waited. Nothing came out. I tried a few more times.

Meanwhile, a security guard approached and said, "Sir, you can't have that poster in here. You'll have to remove it or roll it up."

Stunned and not processing his request, I said, "I'm not trying to make a political statement, I'm just trying to get some cash."

"Let me help you out," he said firm, his voice rising. He pointed to the other side of the courtyard, "Right over there is another cash machine. You can use that one, but roll up the poster."

I didn't dare mess with him. "Okay, I will," I said, rolling up the sign with both hands as I walked. The guard made an erroneous assumption. My poster had merely said, "The Minnesota Delegation Thanks You!" It wasn't a political poster. It was a thank you to the Assembly from the Minnesota caucus for their actions the year before.

A Minnesota delegate had been called to military duty in Afghanistan. Per the idiosyncrasies of Minnesota Law, the substitute teacher who replaced him was paid out of the delegate's teacher salary, meaning the Minnesota delegate took a drastic pay cut to the tune of $13,000.

Fellow delegates at last year's Assembly rose to the occasion and raised the necessary funds out of their own pockets to pay for the substitute's salary. Mark Dayton, Governor of Minnesota, gave the Keynote Address that year and vowed to change the law. He honored his promise and did.

Our posters were a thank you to those delegates who dug deep into their pockets to come up with the $13,000. NEA leadership had given us permission to do this.

Still early in the morning, the strangeness of the guard's request lingered as I walked the maze of hallways towards the Assembly. I stopped at the kiosk to get my overpriced tea. "Who's awake this time of the day?" I asked her. It wasn't a rhetorical question.

She unfurled a sleepy yawn, adding a frown, and said, "Yes. It's way too early." But soon, a big smile broke across her face, the kind you can't make up. In a low voice she said, "I nailed it." She said it the way a student tells a teacher they nailed a big test, and then waits for approval.

It took me a few seconds to process what she was referring to. "Yesss!! Celebration time!" I said, slapping a high-five with her. I had genuine happiness for her success at the audition, even though I didn't know her. Whereas her other auditions had been for minor parts, this was for a lead role; a sultry mistress having a lurid affair with her sister's husband.

In talking with her I discovered that a number of her roles had sultry aspects to it. I suppose directors found this a natural fit for her as she was a slim, attractive, black actress and model with the natural features they look for in a mistress. Yet, you would never figure this from meeting her. She radiated warmth and a down-to-earth, girl-next-door personality that melts you on impact. Her Georgia Peach to my Minnesota Nice transfixed the nature of overpriced teas.

In the end, my natural instincts took over, "You know, we talked about barbeque the other day. Whenever I go on a trip I try out barbeque and interview people for my little YouTube videos. I'm writing a book about all this too. I *know* you're not camera shy. Would you let me interview you?"

"Yes, no problem," she said with a bounce and a smile.

"Great. I'll be back later with my camera and we'll do it when you are not so busy." I don't remember how many teas I bought that day. A lot.

On one of my trips out to the hallway I purchased a ticket to the Mardi Gras Dance later that night, hosted by the Louisiana delegation. Along with my ticket I got colorful beads, which I wore around my neck, adding color to the overcast Fourth of July day.

With each trip to the hallway I scouted the kiosk lines for an opening. I found it later in the afternoon; just the gal, a few workers, and a security guard. "This looks like a good time, right?" I said, holding up my camera.

"Yes."

I felt goosebumps for this would be my first time interviewing a real actor. "Okay, I'll give my little Mr Y BBQ Tour introduction and then I'll turn the camera on you."

She followed my every direction as though I was the best director she'd ever encountered. Estimating her to be in her late twenties or early thirties, I learned in pre-interview rehearsals that she'd been doing plays since age five, giving her a lifetime of acting experience.

I think I looked more like a hiker in the woods than a director. I wore a blue patterned shirt, the one I'd worn to American Idol, over my I BOUGHT A COKE IN AT-LANTA t-shirt. Slap on the beads, add the backpack, and I'm set.

A few adjustments to my camera and I started, "Here I am, Mr Y at the Georgia World Congress Center in Atlanta, Georgia, ... I've been searching for the best bar-beque in Atlanta ... which brings me to the person behind me."

Her bounce and energy took over from there. "Hi. My name is Makeba and I'm originally from Virginia. For barbeque places I love Smithfield's and the Cook-Out," her eyes opened wider with excitement, "both are in North Carolina."

At this point she transitioned. She waved her arms in a short circular motion as thought she had something more to tell. I knew I was on to something bigger than barbeque. Her excitement grew, "I moved here in January for acting and modeling. It's been going pretty well. I started auditioning for movies in May and since then I've booked five. I'm shooting two of them this month, and I had an audition for a lead role yesterday." Now she beamed, "It went really, really well."

I had it, the Interview of the Century with the girl-next-door, the small town girl done good. "Hold it! Hold it! We need to celebrate," I interjected. Bragging rights were mine. Red carpet, here we come.

In smooth synergy we cheered, "Yeah!" She had a flowery, infectious laugh, curling her arms in tight. All together she emanated the sugary sweetness of a ball of honey.

I asked, "Do you like a particular kind of barbeque? Do you like it spicy? You must if you are from the east coast with those vinegar based sauces."

"Yes."

Cut.

I invoked director privilege and got fussy, wanting her to clarify for my viewing audience, however small, where in North Carolina those two barbeque places were. "We're going to need to do another take. Tell us where in North Carolina those two places are."

She handled it like a pro. I'm sure she was used to it. All the directing, all the producing I'd done in my school videos paid rich dividends, preparing me for this moment.

"Say the name of the barbeque places again?" Makeba asked.

"Yes, then tell where in North Carolina they are." I wondered how I compared to other directors. Tough? Easy? Type-A? Type-B?

"Ready?" she asked.

"Yep."

*Click.* "The barbeque places I love are Smithfield's in Fayetteville, North Carolina and ...."

"Is that the northern part near the Virginia border?" I interrupted. I'm always worried about the details.

"No, it's not," she said, not missing a beat. "The Cook-Out is in Greensboro, which is a ways from the border. Smithfield's is further south in Fayetteville." She used defined hand motions to signify north and south.

I swung the camera around to myself. "I've tried barbeque in Raleigh, but now I have another place to go in North Carolina." She stood in the background, curling her arms in tight, giggling and smiling.

When our interview ended she wanted to snap a picture with me. The security guard stood ready to snap away, but I got the sudden urge to take off my blue patterned shirt, revealing only my I HAD A COKE IN ATLANTA t-shirt, and beads.

In the middle of this I heard a brusk voice bark, "She needs to get back to work!" He didn't look happy, the kiosk manager. I looked around, but saw no customers, preparing myself to buy another tea if that would make him happy.

"Oops, sorry," I said, and finished my transformation. I stood next to her ready for the shoot. I could feel her melting warmth, her charm. Irresistible.

I had pursued an interview out of my love for barbeque, but ran headlong into another love. Movies. I watch them, write them, direct them, edit them, and produce them for my school. When a passion triggers, it can't be controlled by any regular means. And now in Atlanta I was in the throes of it. A Star is Born.

Once, my friend and I made a three minute horror flick and entered it in a contest. We called our movie *Three, Three, Three.* We had dead bodies on a remote trail buried in water. We loaded up the special effects, and our crypt-like dialogue in a dark sinister tunnel sent shivers down the spine. Sad to say, the horror of how bad it was far outweighed the horror it was supposed to create.

I had an inkling, so I said to Makeba, "Now watch, some big time Hollywood director who loves barbeque will do a search, find my YouTube video, and see you. Then he'll sign you to a big contract for a blockbuster movie that will sweep the Academy Awards. All I ask is a trip to the Red Carpet."

"You got it," she said.

Before the Assembly ended for the week we had a few more chats, resulting in her giving me her business card. That night I looked her up on Facebook.

The next morning, while ordering tea, in a serious way I said to her, "You're just a go-getter aren't you?"

"Yes, I am. I sure am," she said in a straight tone.

She can tell you why much better than I can:

*I've recently received email requests from people asking me to tell them more about myself. Ok, here goes........ I am an Actress, Model, Falcons Bartender, GA Congress Center Barista, College Grad with three degrees, former Clinical Psych PH.D student, Doggy Mom to my shih tzu, Dior, I truly adore and love my nieces, Khylie and Tori, I have no kids, no boyfriend, I strongly believe my future husband got hit by a bus and died which explains why he hasn't found me yet. I've never had the pleasure of being in love, I'm funny, part time fitness junkie, I have a soft spot for making it rain on the homeless people, nerd, I know the first 30 to 100 digits of Pi, every night I practice my acceptance speech for my Future Oscar win so that when it happens I won't be nervous and take forever to thank everyone.*

*I often pretend I'm getting interviewed by Oprah, sometimes I pray more for my close friends success than I do for mine, and I spend each day trying to do something nice and unforgettable for two people whom I do not know that could never repay me back for the deed I've done. Hope that helps. Thanks for being interested and wanting to know more about me. #me #blessed*

\* \* \*

I'm a fan of Malcolm Gladwell. I've read all five of his

books: *The Tipping Point, Blink, Outliers, What the Dog Saw,* and *David and Goliath.* When I first met Makeba early in the week I made instantaneous decisions about her in what Gladwell refers to in *Blink* as thin-slicing, to use a Gladwellian term.

I sized her up and made assumptions without knowing everything there was to know about her. I pegged her to be the girl-next-door who had moved to Atlanta in pursuit of a dream. Good luck, I thought. Try hard. As an educator I heaped encouragement, given she was a drop of water in a sea of wannabes.

But by the time I left Atlanta my view of her had changed. In Gladwell's book, *Outliers,* he defines an outlier as someone who is "outside ordinary experience." She fits that definition.

Makeba didn't come to Atlanta to make a good go of it. On the outside she might portray the girl-next-door, the small town girl done good, I'll-give-it-my-best. But on the inside she was a different story.

She doesn't believe what the rest of us in conventional society believe. She doesn't fit the mold. She brims with confidence and swag. As President Van Roekel would say, she'll do whatever it takes. She *knows* she's going to make it. If you don't believe me then re-read her little autobiography.

In *Outliers,* Gladwell talks extensively about 10,000 hours. Makeba already had at least 11,000. Her acting range was wide and far reaching—her talents, impeccable. I no longer hoped she would do well. I *knew* she would do well. I *believed* she would do well. I'm already booking my trip to the Red Carpet. I wondered why she chose to go to Atlanta, though, rather than straight to Hollywood. Then it hit me. *Duh,* Tyler Perry.

# CHAPTER 13

During that day's Assembly, Ms. Rinker sat a few chairs away. I said to her, "The concierge recommended Bone Lick BBQ. I like Fox Bros. It's down home Atlanta. I want to go to Thelma's Kitchen, too, but I don't know their hours. The concierge really pushed Bone Lick. She said they're a modern fusion on barbeque."

"Let's go there, "Ms. Rinker said.

I knew I'd be in for a busy Fourth of July evening. First Bone Lick, then Fireworks, followed by the Mardi Gras Dance. Forget about sleep. Our caucus leaders told us to do the work of the Assembly by day, and then go and have fun at night. So I did.

Ms. Rinker and I feared Fourth of July traffic would make it hard to get a cab. It didn't seem bad, although the prickling cab fare of $36 seemed to reflect the special evening.

If you drove by Bone Lick at nighttime looking for barbeque you might drive on past thinking it only a chic neighborhood bar. It sits in an office complex with a nail salon next door. The blue EZ-UP tents outside say *Original Pabst Blue Ribbon Beer* on them. The windows display neon signs advertising various other beer brands, too.

You might not even notice the large poster attached to a tent leg advertising their *$4^{th}$ of July Extravaganza*. But if you looked up, you couldn't miss their retina shrinking, light-up-the-sky sign that said *Bone Lick BBQ* with an outsized arrow.

Ms. Rinker and I entered amid a rush of customers. The place had the tenure of a high end yuppie bar, similar to what I experienced walking around the Old Fourth Ward.

To the right, a long table made from butcher's block took up a majority of space, with traditional booths along the wall behind it.

Sulking above the booths were posters with gyrating Bone Lick themes. For example, one had a drawing of a can of green beans with a label that read, *Bone Lick, Pork Braised Collard Greens*. At the bottom it read, *Finally: A Collard Green that Don't need a Damn Thing*. A hanging barnyard light illuminated each booth, leaving the place with an overall dark feel except where light needed to be.

When we first walked in, I noticed the long bar in front of us with an old time bathtub behind it. Filled with ice, it stood as a clever way to keep cans and bottles cool. The bartenders worked at a crazy pace. A tiny dance floor squeezed between the far end of the bar and the far wall.

Bone Lick BBQ is the fusion of simplicity and sophistication. It's a bar and barbeque crossover. It's not a regular everyday neighborhood bar. Nor is it an exclusive high-end businessman's hangout. Instead, it caters to the twentysomething crowd, who scooped up drinks and created a dinny roar that made it hard to hear.

The host, a skinny thirtysomething Caucasian fellow hustled about like a madman. He informed us of a long wait, and we found ourselves seated at an Atari video game machine.

"You can use the Atari machine as your table if you like," he said.

The menus catered to the chic. Add a touch of Old West, a dash of swanky, a pinch of Yuppie, and we've got something special; colorfully arranged, easy to follow, and appealing.

The combos had their own vernacular: *The Missionary, The Menagé a Trois, The Four Way Biggins*, and *It's The Amazing Fat Ass Sampler*. How cool.

Ms. Rinker proved to be the more daring, ordering *The Menagé a Trois* with its three different meats. I went for my old standby, half-slab ribs.

Somewhere on the menu it said: *Our meats are smoked to perfection using pecan, white oak, & hickory hard woods.* I'd never heard of pecan wood before, which added an intriguing twist. The host ran and jostled, under siege by the burden of making the place hum.

My order arrived in a reasonable time for a place so packed during a major holiday. It came on a rectangular metal tray lined with thin brown paper. It's a chef thing. My salacious half-slab looked yummy, complemented with tater tots, baked beans, coleslaw, and grandly rounded off with Texas Toast.

Texas Toast gave my ribs an outlaw edge. That's how it should be. Barbeque ribs aren't meant for the upper crust, they're meant for the rough and tumble. Tater tots, oh the tater tots. If I were stranded on an island I'd want tater tots.

Ms. Rinker's combo, *The Menagé a Trois,* appealed to me, if only for the sexiness of the name. A conundrum of three meats, in which she delighted in choosing; pork, ribs, and brisket. Her's came with light toasted bread and a small garden salad. The fun arrived in our shared agreement to swap bites of each other's culinary feast.

One roadblock for me, as always, centered around sauces. Indecision is my friend, leaving me to struggle. The choice of sauces were *Wimp Juice* (no heat), *Kansas City* (thick and sweet heat), *North Carolina* (a kick to it), *Mustard* (self-explanatory), and *Big Kahuna* (the hot stuff). I had designs on *Kansas City* sauce as it evoked fond memories of my visit to the city of Kansas City. But in the end I bailed and chose *Wimp Juice.*

Ms. Rinker chowed and chomped. She offered her two cents worth on *The Menagé a Trois,* saying, "The brisket, not as good as Famous Dave's. I liked the ribs, they tasted good. The dry rub was great, and I really liked the pulled pork."

She hesitated in comparing Bone Lick's brisket to Famous Dave's, a Wisconsin born barbeque chain head-quartered out of Minnesota. It's not easy evaluating something eaten for the first time to something eaten more frequently at a familiar hometown establishment. It's not a fair comparison. Tastes and varieties are different and it ends by comparing apples to oranges. The empty void on her plate and her food-stuffed cheeks said more than words ever could.

I loved the smokiness of the ribs. They had that rustic backwoods look immersed in backcountry taste. The coleslaw was so-so, but the beans were dynamite. I could taste and smell the pulled-pork in them. *Yum.* The conspirator in me detected a hint of chili flavor; perhaps a secret ingredient!

The bones were more than generous in size, and had a slight time-delay tangy bite. Not too much and not overwhelming, perfect for someone like me. The tangy bite poked, but didn't prick.

The whole combo delivered rustic perfection, utilizing every weapon of good taste. Ribs, tater tots, coleslaw, and baked beans. They worked together as team players. The blend of exotic flavors made for a fine evening, delivering on the promise of modern fusion for an old staple.

My prior research said the owner had worked as an Executive Chef at a high end restaurant before opening Bone Lick. That much was apparent. The themes and flavors didn't just happen by accident. They were carefully planned with expertise.

I bugged and bothered the host multiple times for an interview. But he succumbed to his many duties, and getting the interview seemed improbable.

In the meantime, Ms. Rinker and I felt the pressure to get back to Olympic Park in time for the fireworks, which required a cab. Our host made the call for us.

Ms. Rinker doesn't like the clamor of crowds. I thrive

in it. As such we headed outside to wait. The night filled with a dim mist. We waited for our cab. And waited. And waited. And waited! I went inside to follow up on the cab, and found the host instead. A moment freed up, and we were on.

Firing up my camera, I said, "Alright, give me your name and what you do here."

"Hi, I'm Mike LaSage, the owner of Bone Lick BBQ, " adding a quick celebratory hand-clap, "and it's the Fourth of July!"

II stood frozen. "Oh! The owner!" This floored me. I thought him to be just an overworked host trying to make the boss look good. I collected myself and continued, pointing to a black woman at the bar, "She's a teacher in Oakland. She's originally from Atlanta and she said she knows the bar owner. That would be you."

"Probably," he said with a grin.

"How long have you owned this place?" I asked, digging for that bit of information that would set my small, but loyal YouTube audience on the edge of their seat.

"It'll be a year next month. A brand new baby back rib barbeque restaurant." Mike rubbed his hands together, like a happy camper at a campfire staying warm.

I had to speak loud to overcome the ever-increasing din of the patrons. I yelled at Mike, "What gave you the idea for this?"

"I love a good barbeque and had a hard time finding the stuff I like, so I finally just opened my own restaurant."

Mike began fading to a shadow on my camera.
A victim of straying from the illumination of the hanging barnyard light above him. "Do me a small favor and take a step that way, under the lights," I said, pointing to a bright spot. He took a step in cooperation.

I probed deeper, "What do you consider your specialty?"

"Everything we do," Mike said, with a crook of a

smile not wanting to concede that one item might get more tender loving care than another. In his mind he slathers equal love on all of it. "We make everything from scratch," adding a quick wave of his hands for emphasis, like an umpire calling a runner safe.

"I read online you guys mix high-end chef stuff with barbeque stuff in a kind of modern feel. Is that correct?" My sentence didn't make complete sense, but I was confident he got it.

"Exactly. Exactly. Putting a new edge on barbeque."

I had one more burning question, "Tell me about the baked beans?"

"The baked beans, we make from scratch. There's more pork than there are beans. Nice and saucy." His beaming reply oozed with smug confidence. His baked beans were a defining pride and joy, a way to beat competitors over the head.

"It seems like they have a little bit of a chili flavor. Is that true or false?"

"A little bit of chili powder in the mix, yes."

"At a lot of places the beans are average. I give your beans way above average."

"We tried to make something a little different."

"It gives them a backwoods feel you expect from barbeque."

"Nothing left to chance."

I have a penchant for researching. I'm possessed by it. If I can gain an ounce of relevant history, enough to impress my friends, I'll do it. I scored some doozies on Mike LaSage and Bone Lick BBQ.

In an ironic twist, at one time Mike was an Executive Chef at a high-end restaurant in none other than the Old Fourth Ward. Yep, that's right. Not a misprint. He started a Barbeque Night every Wednesday. It proved to be a big hit, planting the seeds of Bone Lick BBQ.

I reflected on the fact a mysterious series of interconnected events had occurred that placed me at that exact moment in time at Bone Lick BBQ, talking to Mike LaSage. To begin, I was selected quite at random to Atlanta for the NEA Representative Assembly. Once in Atlanta I decided to visit the Martin Luther King National Historic Site. After touring it, I became determined to make it to the Jimmy Carter Center. In my attempts to find it I got lost and stopped at random in the Old Fourth Ward to find my bearings. Mike LaSage had started a Barbeque Night when he used to work there. Earlier, when I had asked the concierge at the hotel where to eat barbeque she named Bone Lick BBQ. Pushed it. Sold it. Ms. Rinker agreed. Full circle. Those seemingly random series of events weren't random at all. The Chaos Theory at work.

Later in the week I struck up a conversation with another concierge at the Omni. Not the first one I talked to, but a different one. "We went to Bone Lick BBQ," I told her. "Your other concierge recommended it, really pushed it. She even whipped out a promotional card. Said it was the best place she'd been to in town."

This concierge paused, then spoke clear and deliberate, "When Bone Lick opened, the owner brought in all the concierges from area hotels and fed them." Two-and-two make five. Brilliant!

Back at Bone Lick, Ms. Rinker reported that the cab had gotten delayed due to Fourth of July traffic. In the meantime, she struck up a conversation with a bubbly middle-aged gentleman who went by the moniker Duckman. His mustache abetted his round friendly face and good cheer. It turned out he was a Georgia native, and came from a long Georgia family tree.

I made multiple treks inside, and each time I scooted back I found Ms. Rinker and Duckman in spirited laughter. Seems Duckman had a bag full of stories and a knack for storytelling.

Duckman and his wife divorced after twelve years, and they lost the house when "she stopped making house payments." He laughed up a hoot like a person does when a once tragic event has turned comical with the passage of time.

"One, two, three ... go," I told him as I hit the button on my camera.

"Hi. It's Duckman from Georgia," he said in his distinct accent. "I entered a Twinkie contest. I had six in my mouth, but I *swallered* five and a half."

Ms. Rinker couldn't contain herself. I asked Duckman, "Where did that put you in the contest?"

He broke into a gentle soothing grin, raising his right index finger, "First place ...," Ms. Rinker made vain attempts to contain herself, "*and a half.*" She totally lost it.

When I stopped giggling I said to Ms. Rinker, "Where the heck is the cab?"

"I can give you a ride if you need it," Duckman offered.

"No, we're fine, the cab should be here soon," Ms. Rinker replied.

"I'd be happy to give you a ride," Duckman offered again. With time to kill, Duckman shared his thoughts on the state of barbeque in Atlanta. His favorite place? Shane's Ribshack.

We conceded defeat and let Duckman give us a ride. Ironically, as we walked to his truck in the ramp we spotted our cab waiting around the corner. "That's why we never saw it," Ms. Rinker said. "Oh well."

Duckman took to storytelling on the drive back to the hotel, filling us with facts and fun stuff Joe Tourist would never know about. He dropped us off right at the doorstep of our hotel, refusing our offers of money.

Timing is everything. We arrived to the grandeur of the Fireworks Grand Finale over Olympic Park. Duckman stayed and watched right along with us. I didn't fail to note the grandness of the evening or of Olympic Park. Those warm feelings of yesteryear stuck around.

Duckman is one of the good guys. He's a Southern

gentlemen in the truest sense, blessed with the gift of gab and a grand facility for storytelling. Ms. Rinker sure had a hoot. He's the glue that tied the evening together, further proof positive that Southern hospitality is alive and kicking; he could be a poster child for it. In twenty years, when I'm old and gray, I'll still be talking about the night I met Duckman. Somewhere, someplace Ms. Rinker will still be trying to contain herself.

\* \* \*

For Ms. Rinker, after the fireworks, the evening ended. But for me, it just began. I felt as free as a bird and craved some action. After freshening up in my room, I started the long trek to Peachtree street for the Mardi Gras party. Once downtown I navigated the maze of hallways connecting the downtown hotels with the spirit of an explorer. The hallways were illogical and irrational at best. Eventually I made it to the ballroom in the bowels of the Marriott hotel, ready to get it on.

I didn't waste any time in heading straight to the dance floor. I'd been up since 5:45 am and even though the effects of the long day had begun to take its toll, I motored on. I didn't know anyone, although I did recognize a few faces. The great thing is that I didn't need to know anyone. Most people there didn't know anyone.

I grooved to the beat along with all the other delegates running on adrenaline-powered fumes. Delegates packed every inch of the ballroom floor like sardines. I forced myself to revive my old ushering skills again, bobbing and weaving, slipping and sliding.

In some cases I used delegates as human shields to get to random spots on the floor. In other cases they became my defacto blockers, like offensive linemen leading a charge up the middle. The fun is always in the journey, not the destination.

The folks from Louisiana sure knew how to throw a party. They were bonafide masters in the art. They took charge and crowned a King and Queen. They pushed an energy that unraveled common sense, and formed a train dance that snaked and shaked beyond reason. I joined right in. It reminded me of my days at the roller rink doing the hokey pokey. As the train snaked throughout the ballroom, it got longer and longer, leaving no delegate without the opportunity to participate.

The fun ended when I caved in to fatigue and made the forlorn decision to call it a night at 2 am and head back to the hotel. I moved in shuffled steps as I reverse engineered my route.

I found my way to Peachtree street, walking in the direction I needed to go to get to Andrew Young International Blvd., which would lead me back to the hotel. Somewhere near a parking ramp I spotted a group of people I assumed were other delegates walking back from the Mardi Gras party.

I spotted a woman on the tail end of the group, and in the darkness held a ray of hope it might be the delegate from Florida I had so briefly talked to during a break in the Assembly proceedings. I had wanted to talk to her again and thought this might be the moment. I walked faster to catch up.

The woman in the rear stopped, the others heading on. She turned to me as I approached, saying, "Hi honey. How's the evening?"

Dark hair, dark eyes, dark skin and wearing a solid dark dress, she matched the features of the Florida delegate and fit my own personal profile of what I'm attracted to. My knees buckled in the presence of such beauty.

"Oh, hi," I said.

She asked, "Where are you coming from?"

In wholesome innocence I said, "I'm coming from the Mardi Gras party down the block, it's letting out."

"You know, the night's still young, we could have some fun." By now I'd begun to realize this wasn't the

Florida delegate I'd talked to at the Assembly. But en-thralled with this striking woman, I plunged forward. She possessed that sweet Southern accent I gravitate toward and fall in love with.

I said, "Yes, the night is young, but I'm pooped. It's been a long day." By now I had suspicions. Ignorant to the core and naive to a fault, I had an inkling of what the true situation presented. When I pointed in the direction of the Mardi Gras party, she turned to face me with a quick movement, looking both leery and suspicious in the same motion.

Pressing her face to mine, she said, "You know I could come with you and be with you all night long and we could have some fun." A lady of the night was propo-sitioning me. The lure of her breath, her red glimmering lips poised with temptation, preyed on my weakness. My knees buckled, again, in futile resistance.

"Okay, I get what you're saying here. You're certainly an attractive woman," I said in a voice punctuated by trembling. "I'm sure you are a wonderful woman, but my answer is no, I'm going to be a good boy tonight."

She pulled a small bottle of perfume from her purse and sprayed it on her arm, waving it near me. "I could come with you, I could be yours tonight. Smell the scent. Don't you love it? You could experience this all night long. Don't you want to be with me? We can be together."

She pressed her attack, "I can come to your hotel room for a few minutes and give you some fun." I used every fiber in my body to resist, almost, *almost* asking about prices.

Here I was, in a far away land, free as a bird, single, with no cares or concerns in the world. In the wee hours of the night a lady of the night weakens the soul. I *burned* to send purity to the roadside and morality over-board. I tempted to give in, to satisfy my impulses, to seize the opportunity in front of me.

"I'm sure you're a wonderful woman, and you're certainly very attractive and alluring, but I'm going to be a good boy tonight. I know that's disappointing to you." How I found the strength to say this I don't know. I said it as diplomatically as the moment demanded. "I'm sure you're going to do fine tonight. There are a lot of people coming this way from the Mardi Gras party down the block. They're just letting out now. I'm sure you'll find success." I pointed in the direction of the delegates now flooding the streets.

Her arousing scent pushed limits. Her face was still close to mine, our lips almost touching. Our eyes locked as she said, "I love teachers! I'm going to get one tonight!" Her enthusiasm was hard to misplace.

"I'm sorry, I really am," I said. A little Catholic guilt found its way, even in this moment of combustible morality. "But I'm a good boy tonight."

Disappointment and discouragement marred her features. She turned and pointed behind herself. "You say the party just ended and there's a lot of people that way?" suddenly possessing a school girl innocence.

"Oh yes! There are lots of them coming! Business should be good!" I pointed in agreement with her.

A smile rose from her heap of rejection; a glimmer of hope filled her spirit, "Okay, thanks. That way?" she said, pointing again in the direction of the delegates.

"Yes, right up the block. You'll have a great night!"

I pointed one more time, determined to help her like a travel guide helps a tourist. I witnessed her disappear into the darkness. I couldn't think of a better way to get off the hook. Moments away from caving in, I had to do something. Bold situations require bold action, and I had stood my ground.

A small part of me harvested guilt for sending unsuspecting souls to hell, and quite possibly marriage counselors. But another part of me patted myself on the back for holding firm, thus preserving what little of my moral fiber remained. I had doubts as I crossed over Peachtree street. *I should've done it. No I shouldn't have. I should've done it. No I shouldn't have.*

Not far from Olympic Park, a black man approached holding a cardboard sign. He asked for money and gave a story about the plight of his family; they needed to move and he didn't have anything.

I have doubts about these situations. I never know if what I'm donating is really going towards the intended purpose, or towards the purchase of a bottle of whiskey at the nearest liquor store, helping to send the fellow deeper into addiction.

The difference maker here is not what he asked for, but how he asked for it; in genuine humility. It's like he'd read Dale Carnegie's book, *How to Win Friends and Influence People.*

My only explanation is that infused into this man's DNA was the sweet nectar of Southern hospitality. Strange and as wrong as it sounds, even the homeless people in Atlanta are infused with this sweet nectar of Southern hospitality. I gave him $10 out of sheer respect for his request, doing my part to make the world a better place. It was between him and God now, what he does with it.

I reflected on my short walk from Peachtree street, about the two individuals who had asked for money for two different reasons. They each shared a common goal punctuated by a need to survive. Strange, that it was moral to give to one and not the other. I knew right then I had experienced the confounding extremes of our human existence.

# CHAPTER 14

*I should've done it. No I shouldn't have. I should've done it. No I shouldn't have.* Those thoughts percolated with robust strokes the next morning. They soon faded to the background as I staggered down to our caucus meeting. I loaded my plate high with food and poured a glass full of orange juice, and another of apple juice. I determined to stay awake by any means, and food was a proven commodity.

After our caucus meeting I hopped across the street to CNN Center again. I approached a guard, and said, "Hey, the other day I was carrying a poster related to the NEA convention across the street. It wasn't a political poster, but the guard said I had to get rid of it or roll it up. Is it because we're in CNN Center and CNN has to appear nonpolitical because they are a news organization?"

"Yes, that's why," he said. Satisfied, I finished my errand and headed over to the Assembly.

We rambled through more New Business Items and started digging into Legislative Policy and Constitutional items. I found New Business Items more interesting than the other two. They were much easier to understand and were more specific to the classroom; Legislative and Constitutional items were loftier and more big picture.

We held our secret vote on Constitutional Amendment #2. The voting process itself was reminiscent of presidential elections; we had to wait in long lines, show proof of ID, and insert our ballot into the machine in a certain specific way.

I butt in line to dirty looks even though I didn't deserve them. I had followed the instructions of an usher to a tee. He said to take the escalator down and hop in line to "avoid the long wait." He was right.

During the Assembly a curious event happened. The Pacific Islander woman showed up in our Minnesota section. It appeared she knew one of our delegates and was carrying on a conversation.

My analytical brain rationalized in paranoia. I had twice attempted to start a conversation with her earlier in the week and had been rebuffed both times. Now she mysteriously shows up in *my* section. *There must be a connection. She must be communicating with me via karma. There's something to this. This isn't some random thing.*

She appeared in our section multiple times more throughout the day. Each time my attention shifted, and I searched the corridors of my mind for some reasonable, if not logical, explanation.

Beyond that the day for the most part was unremarkable, except for my fatigue. I moved slow. The Assembly ran well past our slated end time of 5 pm. We couldn't leave until the last Item was voted on.

Upon exiting the GWCC after the Assembly ended for the day I determined to be adventurous, walking east into unexplored territory. I had heard there was an ethnic restaurant over there somewhere and I wanted to check it out. I found it in a genuine ethnic neighborhood with the likes of Indian, Italian, Mediterranean restaurants galore and more.

Ethnic restaurants bring a United Nations quality to the community. They bring a world perspective to an area that otherwise wouldn't know any better. It's something I'd experienced overseas and it's wonderful. I remained hungry, though, for they had all closed minutes before my arrival.

I had time to reflect on my walk back to the hotel. The importance of my job as a delegate hadn't really sunk in. It had all moved so fast.

In those few quiet moments I began to understand the impact my votes would have on America, as big as that sounds. I came to the Assembly on a whim, but had performed my duties to the very best of my ability. I considered all arguments before voting. I reasoned with passion and resolve. I took pride in that.

\* \* \*

On Fourth of July I roamed the corridors of the Assembly Hall soaking in all that was festive. There contained a special, celebratory bounce in the step of the delegate. All were in good cheer, and here we were, doing the important work of America. Pride filled our faces and grit laced our votes.

Uncle Sam. Captain America. Looking up I saw it, another icon of American pride and joy; the black stove pipe hat. It rose above the crowd bopping up and down, moving at an unsteady pace. The black coat and pants, the beard, looked all too familiar.

I peered and pondered, and came to the same conclusion as others. Honest Abe Lincoln had decided to grace our Assembly, spreading his reassuring, honest cheer to all who encountered him. America's past, present, and future all accounted for.

Confounded and giddy I approached knowing the moment of opportunity was at hand. I reached into the deep recesses of my pocket and pulled out my smartphone. "Hey, Honest Abe. Could I get a picture with you?" I said.

He lumbered over me, pondering with a sly, gentle grin as only the Rail Splitter could do. Looking at me with those deep, recessed eyes he said, "I'll make a deal with you. I'd be happy to pose for a picture with you if you'll make a donation to the NEA."

"Done!"

\* \* \*

I had volunteered to man the Minnesota booth out in the hallway. NEA elections for leadership positions had been held the previous day. Candidates had gone all out lobbying delegates to vote for them.

But while I sat there, no delegates roamed the hallways. No candidates stumped and lobbied. All signs and posters had been put away. The truth was that the results were in. I was out there all by myself, although Ms. Rinker did come and join me in the silent fun for a while. The few delegates that did straggle by either caved in to my schmoozing or questioned my sanity.

"The elections are over," they proffered, asking, "what are you doing out here?"

"We're hoping for a run-off vote," I replied. "I'm lobbying just in case."

Choosing to schmooze with me meant entering my wheelhouse. I gain energy by talking. Solutions to problems become clearer. Stress and anxiety dwindle. I'm unable to hide the fun I'm having.

A Texas delegate, a black woman, made the giddy decision to schmooze. She hailed from the great city of Houston. In a festive mood befitting the day she wore a fluffy red, white, and blue scarf which highlighted her jean jacket and skirt attire. Perky and fun, she stirred about her favorite barbeque places in Houston.

I first set her in motion by asking, "What's your favorite barbeque place in Houston?"

She pondered and fussed, putting a finger to her chin in thought. But I set a boundary! "You only get to choose one." I said it the way a teacher limits a student to one piece of candy from the jar.

After more *hems and haws* she declared, "The best barbeque ... *mmmm* ... Good Company!"

"I've never heard of it," I said.

"Oooohhhh!" she said, rolling her eyes, releasing her body in dramatic ecstasy.

"Houston is *soooo* spread out," I interjected, "I thought Minneapolis was spread out ... until I went to Houston."

"Come with gas money!" she said with a smile, frisking away.

\* \* \*

On Saturday, the last day of the Assembly, delegates left for home early and often. And looking around at those remaining I wasn't the only one exhausted. A collective lethargy had set in, slooping eyes and bobbing heads were the norm. We didn't get a respite from the devil just because we were tired.

A curious thing happened. The Pacific Islander woman reappeared in *my* section, again, with decided frequency. She arrived so often and stayed so long, an unknowing newcomer would think her a Minnesota delegate.

In a fitful state of paranoia I pleaded for the karma she broadcast to make itself understood. But I also held firm in my unwillingness to make myself known. I had done my part, I thought, and I shouldn't have to do more.

All of us delegates could sense and feel that the end was near. We continued to plod through Item after Item after Item, watching the clock spin without purpose. By midday the auditorium sat half empty.

Internally we each begged in silence for the proceedings to end. Three o'clock, four o'clock, five o'clock, six o'clock. The air slowly seeping out of our lungs. We don't get to leave until the last Item is voted on.

At last ... the final Item. New Business Item 93. The one in opposition to "Redskins" being the name of the Washington Redskins NFL football team; the one that caused so much rancor and rage. The most emotional issue of the Assembly, and it was the very last item.

I had expected more fiery debate, more rage, more rancor, and more emotion. But President Van Roekel made a brilliant offer. He would be willing to write a letter to members of Congress opposing the use of the name "Redskins," and by doing so, if we all agreed, we wouldn't need to take a vote. All of us delegates unanimously agreed with ubiquitous thanks.

Those who left early blew it. *Money!* First, they gave away $10,000. And then $15,000! A few lucky delegates would go home flush with cash. All of a sudden, we perked up. Energy sparked. Tension came alive. The drama, the suspense, the wait, all worth it.

"Will those state delegates whose state starts with the letter *M* please rise," President Van Roekel said. We in the Minnesota delegation shot up from our chairs. "The winner of the $15,000 is a delegate from the state of ...." *Poop*. Well, it was fun.

Speeches. Painful speeches. Lots of them. By those leaving office. By those seeking office. By those winning office. From dignitaries. From friends of dignitaries. From friends of friends of dignitaries. It had the effect of punishment. The clock pushed past 7 o'clock.

Many speakers were full of fire and brimstone. Well-honed and well done. They'd planned their speech for months, preparing in front of mirrors and mock audiences, ready to set a new course for America. Except no one was listening.

Instead, the words just echoed off the black plastic chairs. We who remained didn't care. We only wanted for it to end so we could go home.

On the day the verdict was announced for the Zimmerman trial in Florida, Jay Leno told a joke about George Zimmerman during his *Tonight Show* monologue. After telling the joke Jay stood there expecting a response from the audience. Not a peep emerged. Not a single solitary peep. He just stood there. Stone dead silence. Not a cheer or boo or sigh. Nothing. In all the years I've watched the *Tonight Show*, I've never seen that before.

It was that same way for our speakers. Brutal. Finally, mercifully, the speeches ended. "And now for a highlight video!" President Van Roekel bellowed. I felt the glum of the few remaining delegates. I would know. I was one of them. Each of us wanted to yell "*Division*," or "*Roll Call*," anything to get this to end. But instead, we dutifully watched in boredom. Finally, in an act of mercy, President Van Roekel declared an "end to the NEA." Thank God.

I had one final hope of meeting that Florida delegate again. I had seen her from afar during that day's Assembly and hoped to cross paths with her so I could strike up another conversation. I failed.

Accepting it I scurried along the maze of hallways that lined the GWCC. Future candidates and their supporters lined the corridors shouting and screaming and lobbying as we made our way to the exits. Pushing through the crowds, I saw her, a familiar face, holding up a sign in an attempt to lobby for her candidate of choice. Karma, one more time. I pushed through, head down, not willing to make eye contact. I had done my part, I thought, and I shouldn't have to do more.

It had been a heckuva week. I was a veteran now; no longer green behind the ears. I would tell a first-timer to soak it all up, listen, and for God's sake schmooze. Take advantage of all that is in front of you.

And expect the unexpected. Listen to the debate and make your own decisions. Perhaps, most important of all, vote with passion. You are there to make a difference, and you will. Each person you meet will shape you in some finite way. Be *curious*. Be *inspired*. Be *awed*. Be *humbled*. Be *grateful*. Live the dream baby!

My plan from the beginning had been to stay an extra day, rent a car, and explore. To that end, I woke up Sunday morning with a hangover, even though I don't drink. I had been to the mountain top. But the party was over. I crashed and burned from fatigue. The emotions, the anticipation, the energy, the adrenaline all were in the past. I was back to reality on my own dime.

I lumbered down Peachtree street to the small build-ing that housed Hertz Car Rental. The building looked more like an accountant's office with its compact parking lot and dark cubed structure. I could feel the tension of the other customers waiting in the lobby.

A lone worker, outnumbered and overwhelmed, han-dled them as best she could. I heard rumblings about a worker in back. After a long wait he entered. When my turn came I shuffled up to the counter and said to him, "I'm wondering if I could rent a car for the day. A small subcompact would be great."

He processed what I had said like I had punched him in the gut. "Come on man not a chance. We ain't got noth'n." He expressed a hurt over my even asking.

He succeeded in delivering humiliation. I felt ashamed I had even made the trek. The service at this Hertz location ran in stark opposition to the smooth, effi-cient, professional, courteous service I had received at the airport. I walked out the door a rejected man.

I shuffled down the sidewalk back to my hotel with barely an ounce of energy. A homeless man approached. If I would give him a donation, he would give me a copy of a publication they were distributing.

Like the homeless man I'd encountered the other night, he asked with a humility that made me want to give him a hug. He too had DNA infused with the sweet nectar of Southern hospitality, of which I can no longer explain.

"This isn't much, but I hope it helps ... you have a great day," I said handing him some bills.

"Thank you," he said, accepting my small donation with grace. In that single moment he restored my belief in the human race. I was supposed to be the one picking him up, doling out hope. Instead, he did that for me.

I wondered if he'd occupied a stall in the parking

ramp the other night, one of the homeless people I'd seen on the way back from Turner Field. I hoped not, and internally wished him the best. Silent tears he couldn't see welled in my eyes.

I inquired of the concierge back at the hotel about another car rental company. Enterprise had cars available and could even pick me up. The problem was the $250 for the day. So I went for Plan B instead.

All week long a wide swath of delegates raved about Max Lager's. My goal for the week had been to eat at four barbeque places. I had eaten at three which left one to go. I desperately wanted to finish with Thelma's Kitchen, but they were closed. I found it hard to part with that dream. They were an icon, a hole-in-the-wall, rated the best soul food in Atlanta. But, they were closed.

I had a new problem. I had left my backpack at Bone Lick BBQ a few days earlier. I needed it. The porter hailed a cab and I made the trek to reclaim it. To my good fortune, they had it. I couldn't help but note the cab fare only amounted to $20, which gave me cheer. Ms. Rinker and I got ripped off the other night with the $36 cab fare. I issued a modest complaint with the hotel porter about this.

"We don't control the rates," he said, "it varies greatly by cab company."

Satisfied, I began my trek to Max Lager's. I made the sleepy walk back down to Peachtree street, moving icky and slow. The glum, overcast day didn't help. When I got to Max Lager's I discovered they didn't open until 4 pm.

I killed time in a nearby Starbucks where the perky barista chatted away in her British accent. I wasn't in the mood to talk. I wanted to order a drink, sit down, and vegetate. I listened in pained anguish. She persuaded me to get a medium instead of a small. More profit for Starbucks, I mused.

I wanted to tell her to stop talking, until she said, "You're interesting and intelligent." *Wow!* My attitude turned on a dime. She's a genius, I thought. Starbucks is lucky to have her. She's a good salesman and a pro with the customers.

I struggled to shake the blues though. I made the short walk back over to Max Lager's and got seated by the host. They're housed in a century old warehouse constructed out of bricks and beams.

Damon, my server, was a twentysomething black man about my height and shape. It wasn't hard to convince him to give me an interview. I gave him a short spiel on the Mr Y BBQ Tour and he was all in. He was equal parts personable, knowledgeable, and funny.

He sat across from me with sunny ease. It didn't take long for me to recognize his DNA. "I've been working here about three years," he answered to my inquiry. Pointing to my ribs, he said, "We're a wood fired grilled brewery. First the ribs are smoked for about an hour. Then we take them out of the smoker and grill them on top of hickory and oak wood. When you bite into this, you'll taste the hickory and oak flavor. The ribs are beer basted because in our barbeque sauce we add a little bit of our Max's Red Beer." He pointed to the sides, adding, "These are our hand cut fries and our country coleslaw."

"Does it matter that I'm not a beer drinker?"

His big smile expanded. I got him with that one. "It definitely doesn't matter at all, it adds to the flavor." He said it a bit defensively, but still grinning.

Damon brings an energy any coach would drool over. He's proactive and makes customers like me feel right at home. I began to see my day turn a corner. The glum began to dissipate.

"How long has Max Lager's been here?"

"Max Lager's has been here since 1998, but this building has been here way longer than that."

"Are you a native Atlanta person?"

"No, I'm from Baltimore. I've been living here for about three years. Actually, to make a long story short, I did live here when I was a little kid for a couple of years, then I moved up to Baltimore."

Off camera he filled in the details. He had moved with his family to Baltimore when he was little. He had attended college there and obtained a job based on his degree with the Department of Defense. He got laid off and moved back to Atlanta to be near his mom. He started working at Max Lager's as a waiter, since he had previously worked as a waiter to get through college. He eventually found a job in Atlanta based on his degree, but continues to wait tables on weekends.

"And now you're back," I said.

"Now I'm back. Atlanta's a good place, there's a lot to do. It's a great town. People ask me if we serve Pepsi. I find it funny. I'm like 'Dude, what town are we in?'"

I found it funny, too.

"We have a lot of microbreweries here," he said, matter of fact.

I said, "That's the thing about Minneapolis, especially Northeast Minneapolis. Microbreweries have taken off like you can't believe. Just boom, boom, boom, boom. They're everywhere."

I continued on in an attempt to impress him, "My co-worker told me that ten years ago there were 2200 microbreweries in America. Now, there are over 76,000."

He listened with sheer patience, adding, "On our beer menu we have a couple of beers from the Minneapolis area."

"Really?" Now he had my attention.

I had ordered the half-slab beer basted ribs, French fries, and coleslaw. The half-slab stretched from one side of the plate to the other, coated in a reddish tint. Between the tint and aroma I saw no reason to wait to dig in.

The ribs were tender and fell right off the bone, but not in a traditional way. Characteristically, they were similar to a well-honed roast beef. It's my firmest belief that being both smoked and wood-fired had something to do with it.

The beer basted sauce made it interesting, adding one more thing to hook a customer. Mike LaSage of Bone Lick BBQ might be a little jealous as Max Lager's took a page out of his playbook, adding a new kind of modern fusion to an old staple.

The spice of the ribs and sauce was slight and didn't arrive right away. I could feel the slight beer texture, which added a smoothness not normally found in ribs. If I were a beer drinker, I would give a complete exposition on all the detailed micro-features found in the sauce. But I'm not able to discern the subtleties given my lack of a drinking past. I love it when the slightly spicy flavor arrives in delayed fashion. It's like finding one more present under the Christmas tree.

The coleslaw was billed as country coleslaw, and was as authentic as what grandma used to make. In some versions the cabbage flavor dominates, but that wasn't the case here. The other actors, the supporting cast, got equal playing time. This coleslaw democracy raised the bar on all other coleslaws.

The country seasoning of the fries added a nice variance. A cousin of sorts to the coleslaw. Not a peppery flavor, but special, like when someone adds their secret spice to a dish, but won't tell you what it is.

Damon had to go help other customers. In the meantime another waitress, Morgan, came over to fill the void. I made an inquiry. She assured me she wasn't camera shy. From the second I turned on the camera something about her seemed different. Nothing odd, but I couldn't put my finger on it.

Glib and natural, she gave me the low down. "I'm Morgan. This is Max Lager's, where we brew our own beer. Over here we have our (*undecipherable*) and brewing equipment," pointing behind me. "If you go upstairs we have our serving tanks lined up on this wall," pointing some more. "We have six of them and run lines directly down to our bar. And then we have our fermentation tanks that line the windows on this wall over here," pointing again. "So definitely go upstairs and look at those." From her hand motions, I garnered the serving tanks and fermenters upstairs formed a right angle to each other.

She had used an undecipherable term in that one sentence. *Matched tin? Mashed in?* She said it so matter-of-factly. I'm not a beer drinker and didn't have a clue what she was referring to. I didn't even pick up on it until four months after our interview, when I reviewed the video. I watched it over and over again struggling to identify what the term was. Eventually, I went out to the internet and did a search for like sounding terms. I found a comprehensive beer glossary on craftBeer.com and went to work. After much searching, I found it—I think:

**Mash tun**—*The vessel in which grist is soaked in water and heated in order to convert the starch to sugar and to extract the sugars, colors, flavors, and other solubles from the grist.*

Morgan continued, "The cool thing about being a microbrewery in the city is we bring in a lot of micro-brewery beers from other states. I'm from central New York where we have Southern Tier Brewery and we also have the Middle Ages Brewery up in Syracuse. One of my favorite beers by them is Impaled Ale. Kind of goes along with the whole Middle Ages type idea. I love their Wailing Wench beer, too, and they have a bunch of other ones that are really neat. As far as Southern Tier Brewery, one I've seen the most down here is their 2XIPA. They come out of Lakewood, New York, right outside of Bingham-ton."

I looked up Southern Tier Brewery's website, stcBeer.com. 2XIPA is *An India Pale Ale kicked up a notch to form a true Double IPA*. It's been brewed since

2010 and has an ABV of 8.2 %, whatever that is. According to beerAdvocate.com it has a BA score of 91. I don't know if that's good or bad.

I asked, "Is it fair to say Max Lager's has fused together great food and microbrew?"

"Yes. Since we brew our own beer, obviously, it's our main focus. We do incorporate it into a lot of our foods. Our beef stew often has our Sau in it. We do alternate our beers throughout the year. We have an Oktoberfest fermenting right now. This past week we brought in our Airlift which is a Berliner Weisse. It's a sour beer, German style. It's almost like a German lemonade. We also brought in our Conch, which if anyone has ever been to Cologne, Germany, all they drink is Conch. It's amazing."

I made a pale attempt at comedy, "I've been to Cologne before, but I'm not a beer drinker, so I didn't drink it. Ahaaaah!" I saw the corners of her mouth unfurl the makings of a slight grin.

"It's worth trying," she said. "You can always get one of our samplers. We have samplers of six or seven ... you get a three ounce taste of each beer we have on draft. So you can taste and choose without committing to a whole glass, especially if you're not a beer drinker."

Morgan had to leave for a second for their line-up. Anytime I hear the term, *line-up,* it's cause for concern given my past work history at a juvenile correctional facility.

She put me at ease, explaining it's where the wait staff lines up so management can fill them in on all the important Max Lager's news for the day, upcoming events, specials, etc.

I still puzzled over the fact that something seemed different about her. She seemed exceptionally natural in front of a camera. More so than the average Joe—the way she looked into the lens, her facial expressions, her hand motions. They all had the smooth glide of a professional.

I pressed her on this, "You seem awful natural on

camera. More so than most people I interview. Have you done this before?"

She broke into an earthy smile. "Yes I have. My mom works in journalism and film. She would recruit me and my friends to be on camera while she made her documentaries. So I got comfortable being on camera. I worked as a DJ at my college radio station and worked as the program director too."

"Are you going to work in journalism like your mom?"

"I want to work in TV and journalism, but the opportunities in Atlanta are limited, and you have to be connected to the network of insiders to get a job."

She is gifted and natural, and it's my belief that in the ecosystem of TV and journalism, they'll find a place for a talented individual like her.

Soon our conversation turned to books. I love books and she does too. What particularly sets her on fire are audio books.

She could hardly contain herself, saying, "You should get a subscription to audio books. I use an app on my iPhone to listen to books and it's how I get my subscription to audio books! I can listen to as many books as I want to and it doesn't cost much."

I said, "That's not a bad way to go. I've not really tried audio books much. I don't like eBooks very much either, even though the book I'm writing will be an eBook. I'm old fashioned; I still like my hardcopy. I like being able to touch it and feel it. I like marking it up as much as I want. I like the sensation of removing it from my backpack and flipping through the pages while I'm lying under the shade of a tree on a sunny day.

I'm on a computer a lot as it is and I don't want to be on one more. That's why I'm not an engineer anymore. I couldn't take the computer screens."

"I don't like eBooks either. I get headaches if I'm on a computer too much. That's why I switched to audio books. I can listen to them while I drive. It's so much cheaper. A subscription is the way to go because you can listen to as many as you want and it doesn't cost you more. That's why I have the app. You should look into it!"

Audio books are now on my radar.

"You have an easy name to pronounce. *Morgan.* I have a hard one," I said, changing gears.

Holding my credit card for payment, she took a quick look at it and said, "*YARN-O.*"

I was both amused and stunned. "You said my name correctly the first time. Very few are able to do that. How'd you know how to say it?"

"I've worked here eleven years and I got good at names. Also, my brother studies French and he practices with me, so I got to practice French names."

"Incredible. My last name is spelled Y.E.A.R.N.E.A.U. It's a French name prone to mispronunciation. I've heard anywhere from *urinal* to *yedrino*. I've had K, X, and W added to my name, yet my name doesn't contain any of those letters.

Most people take an English approach and try to say every letter and butcher it. I usually correct them and give them a hint. I say something like, 'No, no, no. Tim Yearneau, Jacques Cousteau. The E.A.U. is pronounced like an O.' This registers. I finish by telling them, 'You pronounce my name, YARN-O. Say the word YARN,' I start pretending to knit as a visual, 'and add an O ... YARN-O.' They almost always say, 'Oh, oh, oh, okay, now I get it.'"

\* \* \*

I had entered Max Lager's in a glum mood. Once inside, I transformed; lost energy returned and a bounce lifted my spirit. Damon and Morgan did more than serve my food and give good conversation. They made my day whole. They took what little I offered and multiplied it into memorable moments.

I learned about micro-beers and beer basted ribs. Woods, smokers and wood-fired grilling, too. But I didn't stop there, I also learned about audio books and apps and moms and brothers and speaking French. When I had first sat down, I couldn't have guessed all the things I would learn that day.

Two people, strangers if you will, shared their life stories with me. They didn't have to, but they did. Each of them could have smiled, taken my order, served it, wished me a nice day, collected my tip and that would have been that. But they didn't. Instead, they poured their hearts out. They left me smiling and happy and sitting upright, hanging on their every word. *Thank you.*

# CHAPTER 15

Leaving Max Lager's, the clouds of doom had lifted and the skies opened. Staggering towards me through the sunshine, a tall white gentleman approached. Wearing a blue baseball hat, blue jeans, and yellow t-shirt, he said, "Hey man, you got any money you can give me? I'm an alcoholic, man. I got the shakes. I need a drink bad, man. I need help. I'm gett'n dizzy, man. I'm an addict. I got problems. I just need some money, man. Can you help me out?"

Instinctively I reached in my pocket, pulled out $2, and handed it to him, not quite listening to everything he told me. Just then a quick worry struck: I smelled alcohol on his breath. Concerned, I looked up at him, "I hope you're not going to use this to go get a drink ... *are you?*"

"I am, man. That's what I told you! I'm an alcoholic, man. I need a drink. I got the shakes. I need something." He paused for a second to process. "I'll give you your money back if you want me to, man."

I paused for a second myself, processing this new input. "No, that's okay," but I still had doubts. "You have to promise me you'll get help. We all have struggles. Promise me you'll at least try."

"Okay, man, I'll at least try." He looked to the corner of the block and saw a couple of men. "Oh no. Those look like police. I hope they don't arrest me. I don't want to be in this state."

I walked on, leaving him behind. Strange. Even this man, this addict, this alcoholic possessed that DNA full of the sweet nectar of Southern hospitality.

I can think of no other spot in this world where a drunk man would offer to refund the money I'd just given him that he intended to use for a drink. I hoped in silence that I'd made a difference in some small way, though it didn't seem apparent. It's between him and God now, what he does with it.

The cast of characters didn't cease. Further along on my walk, I observed a tall trim black man in a pristine dark brown pinstripe suit, derby hat, cane, and knee length bright orange knickers. Where else but Atlanta, I thought.

I still had hunger pangs, knowing I would be flying home to Minneapolis later that night. I made one final stop at Salad Sensations in CNN Center. It was my defacto lunch spot during the Assembly. I had been determined to trim the calories and stay fit. I had stood in line during peak lunch times for minutes on end. In each instance I was forced to snake around an army of kiosks that stretched to infinity.

Empty now, CNN Center was a ghost town, and I the lone customer. During the convention a cute young Ethiopian girl had served my salads. She was perhaps only a bit older than some of the elementary students I used to tutor. Her youthful smile and innocent enthusiasm added a brightness the lights couldn't provide.

Now, she worried and stressed when she added Ranch dressing instead of French dressing. "It's all good," I assured her, waiting in patience while she made the switch, appreciative of the little ways she made my trip to Atlanta wonderful.

I headed back to the hotel room, grabbed my stuffed-to-the-max backpack, walked down to the lobby, and checked out. The excitement I had felt in the beginning, gone. Going home now.

With the heat and humidity having returned I sweated and huffed as I made my way to the MARTA station some distance away.

Sitting in my seat on the train ride to the airport, I had too much time to reflect. I felt the loneliness of my inner thoughts as the events of the week seemed a distant past.

The MARTA cuts through some of the worst areas in Atlanta; rows of crumbled houses and dark neighborhoods. Seeing those brought back images of the gut wrenching scene I'd observed at the parking ramp. In contrast, I reflected about the custom homes in that upscale neighborhood in Alpharetta. It didn't seem fair. I, too, had experienced the life of luxury, albeit for a short period of time: 5-star hotel, room service, exotic breakfasts, ribs galore, the works. Did I deserve it? I don't know.

But I'd done my part to make the world a better place. I voted with passion and heart. I helped where I could. I added to the archives of the Mr Y BBQ Tour. I had more material, more footage, and more stories. I'd been privileged to arrive, to experience, to meet, to vote, to create, and to listen. The only thing left to do now is to tell.

# The End

###

If you enjoyed my book won't you please take the time to leave me a review at your favorite retailer?

# acknowledgments

I want to thank my editors Delores Topliff and Ghazal Ghazi, whose job it was to keep me in line! More thanks to Ann Wiener for her insightful comments and unbending patience. Bridget Turner, your feedback on the cover design was invaluable. I wish to also thank my sister Jenny Yearneau for her wordsmithing. And the encouraging words of Paul Bennett and Sherrie Dewey can never be underestimated, and they inspired me to keep moving forward. I thank all whom I met in my journeys and were gracious enough to talk to me.